CW01198022

'This book of Advent devotions takes us along a kind of Emmaus Road journey, showing us how all the Scriptures lead to Jesus. Rich in both exegesis and biblical theology, this book will nourish your soul and inspire your wonder.'
Steve Auld, Senior Pastor of Great Victoria Street Baptist Church, Belfast

'Dr Hayward's delightful book is a true adventure, drilling deep and wide into the biblical journey of Jesus' birth. He faithfully weaves together the fulfilled promises of the Old Testament of the Word become flesh, and illuminates the revealed purposes of Jesus Christ: the Deliverer, the Anointed King, the Separated One and the Redeemer. Dr Hayward challenges us to welcome Christ "not as a guest, on the periphery of our lives, but as the closest of family".'
David Burrowes, former MP for Enfield Southgate and Director of the Conservative Christian Fellowship

'Many of us are used to hearing that Christmas is not primarily about presents, turkey and tinsel, but about the birth of Jesus Christ. Could there be a better way of discovering the real meaning of Christmas than following God's plan to prepare for this history-changing birth through the pages of the Bible? This is exactly what John Hayward's book helps us to do. Anyone reading his thoughtful and accessible book through the season of Advent will certainly put Christ back into Christmas.'
Bronwen Cleaver, Director, Institute for Bible Translation, Russia/CIS

'*Rediscovering the Magic of Christmas* is engaging and challenging. The detailed discussion of the Old Testament is interwoven with references to the realities recorded in the New Testament – all highlighting the theme of the Nativity. Rich in spiritual inspiration, academic information and profound insights, the book also contains many helpful challenges! I strongly recommend this brilliant book as a very readable and engaging source of information and inspiration.'
Baroness Caroline Cox of Queensbury, Founder President of Humanitarian Aid Relief Trust (HART UK)

'In preparation for Christmas, John Hayward invites us deep into the wells of Scripture to journey from Genesis to Revelation. In this season of gifts and giving, may we enjoy the "free gift of the water of life" (Revelation 22).'
Rt Revd Dr Jill Duff, Anglican Bishop of Lancaster

'Written with the wisdom of a scholar and the heart of a father, John Hayward has taken the well-loved Christmas story and added depth and warmth. Steeped in familiar traditions and fresh insights, *Rediscovering the Magic of Christmas* brings thoughtful reflection and enlightened understanding to Advent, restoring the magic of the season. This book of daily devotions enriches the anticipation of Christmas and guides the reader closer to the meaning of the manger – the birth of the Christ child – who is the Saviour of the world.'
Peggy Grande, US author, television commentator and opinion writer

'C. S. Lewis once wrote that he did not particularly enjoy devotional books, and much preferred books of theology. John Hayward has written a wonderful devotional which is theologically rich and theologically informed – a book that is both devotional and theological. I am happy to recommend his volume, and trust that many will benefit from this thoughtful work, which begins in Genesis and ends in Revelation, and all throughout points the reader to Christ.'
Bradley G. Green, Professor of Theological Studies, Union University, Jackson, TN

'During the Advent season we all expect a miracle. In this book, Dr John Hayward reminds us of the magic of Christmas: the birth of our Saviour, Jesus Christ. Let this book be your guide to adventure this Advent season. It's guaranteed to melt cold hearts.'
Igor Ionov, Pastor of the Tyumen Holy Trinity Evangelical Reformed Church, Secretary General of the Evangelical Reformed Church (Russia), and Chairman of the Russian Communion of Reformed and Presbyterian Churches

'This is a refreshing Christmas read. It is written intelligently and with a good focus on the great storylines of Scripture. I don't know of anything comparable.'
Dr Dirk Jongkind, Academic Vice Principal and Senior Research Fellow in New Testament Text and Language at Tyndale House, Cambridge

'A marvellous grasp of the interrelated texts of Scripture, showing how they point to and amplify our understanding of the arrival of Christ. It traces the theme of life in the salvation history of the Bible; a theme neglected, I think, in sermons and biblical literature, but absolutely central (and thrilling). John writes elegantly and engagingly, stimulating my interest, which is not an easy accomplishment!'
Dr Tim Savage, International Director of The Gospel Coalition and former Senior Pastor of Camelback Bible Church, Arizona

'What a feast of Scripture, living commentary and application as we journey through Advent – or indeed any time of year. John's wisdom and passion for "healing the world" bring a rich insight to every passage. I shall be rereading next year (and beyond), and sharing with our children and grandchildren, and their friends. I pray it will open hearts and minds to the significance of the costliest, most precious, of Christmas gifts.'
Canon Sarah Snyder, Founding Director of Rose Castle Foundation and former Reconciliation Advisor to the Archbishop of Canterbury

'We prepare for Christmas weeks, sometimes months, in advance. We get a tree, decorate it with ornaments and place gifts under it. We put up coloured lights, "deck the halls with boughs of holly", bake cookies and treats, and fill the house with the scent of cider and cinnamon. Maybe we even have a nativity scene. But how much time do we actually devote to preparing our hearts for the coming of the Saviour? How much effort do we give to opening God's word and learning why it is the Christ child was needed?

How stale has our routine of Christmas activities and traditions become?

'John Hayward addresses these concerns and more by offering this wonderful nativity guide to help us all "rediscover the magic of Christmas". He takes us back to the beginning, in Genesis, leads us through the prophets, arrives at the birth, and then sees it through to Revelation. This book will bless individuals, families and churches, helping one and all to rekindle the true meaning of Christmas.'

Jay Underwood, Lead Pastor, Calvary Bible Church, Burbank, CA

John Hayward has been an active member of Eden Baptist Church, Cambridge, since the early 1990s. He and his wife also enjoy fellowship with Calvary Bible Church in Burbank, California. He holds postgraduate degrees from Cambridge University and Azusa Pacific University. Throughout his career, he has promoted freedom, strengthened democracy and empowered disadvantaged communities. This has included cross-cultural work in Central Asia, directing the Jubilee Centre in the UK, delivering training across Africa, and teaching in churches and Christian universities in the UK and the USA. A lifelong writer – from foreign-language textbooks to newspaper op-eds and UK policy reports – this is his first devotional book.

REDISCOVERING THE MAGIC OF CHRISTMAS

An Advent adventure from
Genesis to Revelation

Dr John Hayward

ivp

INTER-VARSITY PRESS
SPCK Group, The Record Hall, 16–16A Baldwin's Gardens, London, EC1N 7RJ
Email: ivp@ivpbooks.com
Website: www.ivpbooks.com

© John Hayward, 2024

John Hayward has asserted his right under the Copyright, Designs and Patents Act 1988 to be identified as author of this work.

All rights reserved. No part of this publication may be reproduced, stored in a retrieval system, or transmitted, in any form or by any means, electronic, mechanical, photocopying, recording or otherwise, without the prior permission of the publisher or the Copyright Licensing Agency.

Unless otherwise noted, Scripture quotations are taken from The Holy Bible, New International Version (Anglicized edition). Copyright © 1979, 1984, 2011 by Biblica. Used by permission of Hodder & Stoughton Ltd, an Hachette UK company. All rights reserved. 'NIV' is a registered trademark of Biblica. UK trademark number 1448790.

Scripture quotations marked 'ESV' are from the ESV Bible (The Holy Bible, Anglicized), copyright © 2001 by Crossway, a publishing ministry of Good News Publishers. Used by permission. All rights reserved.

Scripture quotations marked 'KJV' are from the Authorized Version of the Bible (The King James Bible), the rights in which are vested in the Crown, are reproduced by permission of the Crown's Patentee, Cambridge University Press.

First published 2024

British Library Cataloguing-in-Publication Data
A catalogue record for this book is available from the British Library.

ISBN: 978-1-78974-514-6
eBook ISBN: 978-1-78974-515-3

Set in 11/14 Minion Pro
Typeset in Great Britain by Fakenham Prepress Solutions, Fakenham, Norfolk
Printed in Great Britain by Clays Ltd, Bungay, Suffolk

Inter-Varsity Press publishes Christian books that are true to the Bible and that communicate the gospel, develop discipleship and strengthen the Church for its mission in the world.

IVP originated within the Inter-Varsity Fellowship, now the Universities and Colleges Christian Fellowship, a student movement connecting Christian Unions in universities and colleges throughout Great Britain, and a member movement of the International Fellowship of Evangelical Students. Website: www.uccf.org.uk. That historic association is maintained, and all senior IVP staff and committee members subscribe to the UCCF Basis of Faith.

For

Dick Dowsett,
a man 'filled with the Holy Spirit'
whose life faithfully 'displays the glory of Christ'
(Acts 2:4; 2 Corinthians 4:4)

Contents

Introduction ... 1

Day 1: In the beginning ... 3
Day 2: A miraculous birth ... 8
Day 3: Out of Egypt ... 13
Day 4: The life of the world ... 18
Day 5: The Christmas donkey ... 23
Day 6: A prophet like Moses ... 30
Day 7: The Nazirite ... 35
Day 8: Reversal of fortunes ... 41
Day 9: O holy night! ... 49
Day 10: A testimony of warning ... 56
Day 11: The coming Redeemer ... 62
Day 12: Twisted lyrics ... 69
Day 13: A new hope ... 76
Day 14: The messenger ... 84
Day 15: The dreamer ... 92
Day 16: The blessing ... 98
Day 17: The manger ... 105
Day 18: Glory, glory, alleluia! ... 114
Day 19: Purification and praise ... 123
Day 20: God's dwelling-place ... 129
Day 21: Another Christmas night ... 137
Day 22: Free at last ... 143

Contents

Day 23: Interchange in Christ	149
Day 24: The great red dragon	155
Day 25: Christmas epilogue	164
Acknowledgements	166
Index of Scripture references	169
Index of non-biblical names	178

Introduction

'Believe in the magic of Christmas' declared the sign nailed to the wall. Incongruously, the setting was a family-run Mexican restaurant in the midsummer heat of California.

For many of us, just the thought of Christmas dinner – with all its rich tastes and smells – is enough to reawaken the taste buds and bring fond memories to mind. Yet, if we are honest with ourselves, many of us have lost the wonder of Christmas that we once knew as children or as new believers. For others, recent bereavement or ongoing struggles may mean the very thought of Christmas fills us with dread.

Rather than stirring our sense of awe and reawakening our faith, our annual encounter with the nativity can often seem stale. Each year, we tend to hear the same Bible readings and, let's be honest, what feels like the same sermons as every previous year. We know that it is supposed to be a magical time, but it has become all too familiar. While our hearts can still be warmed by our favourite Christmas carols (such as 'O Come, All Ye Faithful' or 'Hark! The Herald Angels Sing') and our heartstrings pulled by classic Christmas films (such as *A Christmas Carol* or Frank Capra's *It's a Wonderful Life*), Christmas itself has become wrapped up in far too many cultural and family traditions.

In these pages, I want to rediscover some of the magic of Christmas by feasting richly on several passages of Scripture that are less commonly associated with our celebrations of the birth of Jesus. Initially, these reflections were compiled for the benefit of my adult children – daily Advent verses shared with them while they were away at university. As you join us on our adventure, from Genesis to Revelation, my hope is that one or more of the meditations may help you and others to believe

Introduction

again in the 'magic' – or rather, the awe-inspiring wonder – of Christmas.

Perhaps we will even rediscover, as the sign in that restaurant suggested, that the story of the Christ-child and his mother is not tied to any particular time of year, to the traditions of any particular nation or to our present circumstances. Released from the burden of overfamiliarity, perhaps we will even glimpse afresh the authentic Christmas gift that is for every person, every nation and every day of the year.

My daughter suggests keeping a Bible open at the main text each day and looking up the other referenced passages too. She advises 'spending time to consider the depths of the passages and personal implications'. Recognising that not everyone will have the time or inclination to do this every day, I have included a 'quick glance' for each day. This can serve as an alternative to in-depth reflection or as an introduction to help give an idea of what follows. If you want to avoid any spoilers, you can also skip it. I've mostly quoted from the New International Version, and occasionally the English Standard Version, unless indicated otherwise; any italics, underlining or bold font present in Scripture quotations is my own addition for purposes of emphasis or comparison. Each day's devotion concludes with a couple of questions to help you consider its relevance for your own life. For, as the Scottish natural scientist and evangelist Henry Drummond once observed: 'the great end of reading ... is not what you will get in an author, but what the author will enable you to find in yourself'.[1]

---

1 George Adam Smith, *The Life of Henry Drummond (1851–1897): A shortened version of the biography by George Adam Smith*, ed. Ian Sinclair (Stirling: Drummond Trust, 1997; abridged version of 1899 edn), p. 35.

Day 1
In the beginning

The LORD God said to the serpent,

> 'Because you have done this,
>   cursed are you above all livestock
>   and above all beasts of the field;
> on your belly you shall go,
>   and dust you shall eat
>   all the days of your life.
> I will put enmity between you and the woman,
>   and between your offspring and her offspring;
> he shall bruise your head,
>   and you shall bruise his heel.'
> (Genesis 3:14–15 ESV)

Quick glance

When people first spread the word about Jesus, they did not say they had found 'him whose birth was announced by angels, and whom the shepherds and also the magi visited, Jesus of Bethlehem, the son of Mary'. Rather, they said they had found 'him of whom Moses in the Law and also the prophets wrote, Jesus of Nazareth, the son of Joseph'. So we too must begin with the Law and the Prophets. In Genesis we learn that 'sin came into the world through one man, and death through sin, and so death spread to all [human beings]' (Romans 5:12 ESV). Yet God also repeatedly revealed in the Old Testament that one day a deliverer would come. If we are to rediscover the 'magic' of Christmas, we must first grasp again that the story begins with a curse. We will only

Day 1

feel a sense of awe if we first remember why it was necessary for Christ to come.

In-depth reflection

When Jesus began calling his disciples to follow him, they excitedly told their friends: 'We have found him of whom Moses in the Law and also the prophets wrote, Jesus of Nazareth, the son of Joseph' (John 1:45 ESV). Their understanding of who he was began, not with tales told by their parents featuring angels and shepherds and magi, but with the Law of Moses and the Prophets.

This might appear somewhat odd to us. Many centuries had passed since Israel's former supernatural encounters with God. So we might have expected that the stories surrounding Jesus' birth would define his public profile into adulthood. After all, we know that the shepherds 'made known the saying that had been told them [by the angels] concerning this child. And all who heard it wondered at what the shepherds told them' (Luke 2:17–18 ESV).

We also know that eight days later, after Jesus was presented in the Temple, Anna the prophetess spoke about him 'to all who were looking forward to the redemption of Jerusalem' (Luke 2:38). So the stories that are recorded for us about the events surrounding the birth of Christ were clearly in common circulation.

Yet, when people described Jesus, they did not talk about 'him whose birth was announced by angels, and whom the shepherds and also the magi visited, Jesus of Bethlehem, the son of Mary'. Rather, they talked about 'him of whom Moses in the Law and also the prophets wrote, Jesus of Nazareth, the son of Joseph'. The identity of Jesus thus begins with the Law of Moses.

Jesus himself later taught that 'everything must be fulfilled that is written about me in the Law of Moses, the Prophets and the Psalms' (Luke 24:44). Luke also tells us that 'the Law and the Prophets were until John' (Luke 16:16 ESV). So, to rediscover the original 'magic' of Christmas, we too must return to the time before John and begin with the Law and the Prophets.

In the beginning

When the account of the creation of the space-time universe begins, in Genesis, we are told that 'God saw all that he had made, and it was very good' (Genesis 1:31).[1] It was not long, however, before the earth became 'corrupt in God's sight' (Genesis 6:11). Having initially been created in God's image, Adam was led to question God's benevolent authority. The Bible consistently presents Adam both as the first human (e.g. 1 Chronicles 1:1; Jude 14) and as representative of all humankind (e.g. 1 Corinthians 15:22, 45). Consequently, when he rejected God, so did we all. Thus we learn that 'sin came into the world through one man, and death through sin, and so death spread to all [human beings]' (Romans 5:12 ESV).

The one responsible for leading humankind astray is initially portrayed as a serpent. Later in Scripture he is identified as 'the accuser', 'the adversary' or, in the original Hebrew, 'the satan' (e.g. Job 1 – 2). In the New Testament he is also called 'the devil' or, in the original Greek, 'the slanderer' (e.g. compare the translation of the same word in 1 Timothy 3:6–7 with 3:11, and 2 Timothy 2:26 with 3:3).

Here in the beginning of the Law, immediately after humankind's fall from grace, the Lord God reveals that the woman's offspring will one day bruise the serpent's head. Until that time comes, sin and death will prevail. The Old Testament repeatedly records people's failed attempts to improve the world and restore our relationship with God by our own efforts. Yet God also repeatedly revealed that one day a deliverer would come. Then, 'as by the one man's disobedience the many were made sinners, so by the one man's obedience the many will be made righteous' (Romans 5:19 ESV).

So, if we are to rediscover the 'magic' of Christmas, we must first grasp again that the story begins with a curse. We will only feel a

---

[1] The German theologian Ernst Troeltsch wrote that creation is 'concerned with God's eternal activity of positing the world as a whole, not with the world's beginning'. It is 'not to be understood as an event in time, but rather as eternal creation in the sense that in every moment the world is set forth anew by God'. Ernst Troeltsch, *The Christian Faith: Based on lectures delivered at the University of Heidelberg in 1912 and 1913*, tr. Garrett Paul (Minneapolis, MN: Augsburg Fortress, 1991), pp. 200, 202.

Day 1

sense of awe if we first remember why it was necessary for Christ to come. And we will only recognise how great a blessing his coming is if we first recognise the need for divine intervention in the course of history – and our own need for divine intervention in our lives.

Until my second year at university, I held to the common opinion that most people are, at heart, essentially morally good and motivated by good intentions. I believed that only a small proportion of individuals had bad intentions and might be called 'bad' or even 'wicked'. The more I paid attention to what went on in the world, however, the more I came to recognise that 'badness' is not limited to isolated villains such as mass murderers or rapists.

Daily news reports reinforced the premeditated cruelty portrayed in historical films released in the 1980s such as *Mississippi Burning*, *Music Box* and *Cry Freedom*. With their depictions of racial violence in the American South, ethnic cleansing by the Nazis, and the brutality of apartheid in South Africa, I gradually came to accept that instances of 'wickedness' can be found in almost all people and in all places, at all times. Before long I realised that, according to the standards of my own conscience, even I fell short of what might commonly be described as 'good'. I began to wonder whether there was anyone upright to be found in all humanity. Presumably, even seemingly moral figures, such as Mahatma Gandhi or Mother Teresa, had moments of weakness and selfishness. In the words of Paul, 'the requirements of the law are written on our hearts' and 'our consciences also bear witness, and our thoughts sometimes accuse us and at other times even defend us' (see Romans 2:15). For 'there is no one who does good, not even one' (Romans 3:12).

Ultimately, we probably all like to think the best of others because we also like to think the best of ourselves. It would be too unsettling to think that almost everybody around us considers their own interests to be more important than those of others – than those of our own. Such reassurance, however, offers only false comfort. Like us – like me – every other person is equally self-centred and spends most of their time thinking about themselves, their own hopes and plans, their own memories and regrets. At best, our concerns typically extend no further than those in our closest circles, our immediate families and any others whom we love.

Yet it is this very insight – that humankind is corrupt – that enables us to understand the miracle – and 'magic' – of Christmas. For me, it was as though someone had turned a light on in a darkened room. The eyes of my mind were opened to a whole new world that I had never previously noticed. Collectively and individually, we are cursed. For this reason, 'God [sent] his Son into the world ... in order that the world might be saved through him' (John 3:17 ESV). It is only when we can say, like the apostle Paul, 'I do not do the good I want, but the evil I do not want is what I keep on doing', that we are also able to give thanks to God 'through Jesus Christ our Lord' for delivering us 'from this body of death' (Romans 7:19, 24–5 ESV)!

Pause to ponder

- Think of times when your conscience has 'sometimes accused and at other times even defended' you. To what extent have such instances prompted you to reflect on God's goodness and mercy?
- Who do *you* understand Jesus to be? What difference does his coming make to how you view the problems in the world – and in your own life?

Day 2
A miraculous birth

God said to Abraham, 'As for Sarai your wife, you shall not call her name Sarai, but Sarah shall be her name. I will bless her, and moreover, I will give you a son by her. I will bless her, and she shall become nations; kings of peoples shall come from her ... Sarah your wife shall bear you a son, and you shall call his name Isaac. I will establish my covenant with him as an everlasting covenant for his offspring after him.'
(Genesis 17:15–16, 19 ESV)

Quick glance

From Abram and his wife Sarai in Genesis, through Manoah the Danite and his wife in Judges, to Hannah and Elkanah the Ephraimites in 1 Samuel, we repeatedly see another important thread of the Christmas story: a childless couple to whom a divine messenger foretells the miraculous birth of a son who will play a significant role in God's purposes for his chosen people. Isaiah the prophet later foretells the miraculous birth of 'Immanuel' – whose name means 'God with us'. As explained in Matthew, this prophecy ultimately referred to Jesus the Messiah. Thus, the Law of Moses and the Prophets had prepared the people of God – and us – to expect the miraculous birth of a future deliverer, 'that we might live through him'. The story of Christmas begins with the curse of sin and death; but it continues with a promise of life.

In-depth reflection

We have seen that the Christmas story begins in Genesis 3 with a universal curse that brings death to all. The next eight chapters of Genesis chronicle humankind's consistent rejection of our creator and his good intentions for us. They span the murderous actions of Adam's firstborn son, Cain (Genesis 4); they record God's regret and grief that 'every intention of the thoughts of [the human] heart was only evil continually' (Genesis 6:5–6 ESV), leading to the destruction of all but Noah's family in the Flood; and they culminate with people's self-seeking ambitions at the tower of Babel, resulting in the dispersal of the nations (Genesis 11:1–9).

This, then, is the reason why 'God sent his Son into the world': 'that we might live through him' (1 John 4:9). Yet, before we rush ahead to the birth of Jesus, the Law and the Prophets wish to prepare us for another important thread of the Christmas story: the miraculous birth of a future deliverer foretold by divine messengers.

This thread begins with Abram and his wife Sarai. After stressing that 'Sarai was barren; she had no child' (Genesis 11:30 ESV), the narrative immediately records God's promise to Abraham that 'I will make you into a great nation' and 'all peoples on earth will be blessed through you' (Genesis 12:2–3).

Over the decades that followed, the Lord appeared several times to Abraham. Each time, he revealed further details of his plan. Yet, each time, these promises seemed incredible to Abraham and his wife. Consider his response when God told him that he should call his wife Sarah (meaning 'princess') because she would give him a son and that nations and kings would come from her.[1] 'Abraham fell on his face and laughed and said to himself, "Shall a child be born to a man who is a hundred years old? Shall Sarah, who is ninety years old, bear a child?"' (Genesis 17:17 ESV).

---

1 Christopher Eames, 'What Does the Name "Sarai" Really Mean?', Armstrong Institute of Biblical Archaeology, 21 December 2022: https://armstronginstitute.org/818-what-does-the-name-sarai-really-mean (accessed 19 February 2024).

Day 2

Sarah, too, found God's promises too far-fetched to be believed. When she overheard the Lord, appearing in the form of three men, again tell Abraham that she would give him a son within one year, she 'laughed to herself, saying, "After I am worn out, and my lord is old, shall I have pleasure?"' (Genesis 18:12 ESV).

This particular episode is noteworthy in that we can recognise various features that recur later in the history of God's dealings with humankind. For instance, in Judges 13 we are told about the wife of a certain man, Manoah of the tribe of the Danites, who 'was barren and had no children'. The angel of the Lord appeared to her, saying, 'Behold, you are barren and have not borne children, but you shall conceive and bear a son' (Judges 13:2–3 ESV).

In both cases, we have a childless couple to whom a divine messenger foretells the birth of a son who will play a significant role in God's purposes for his chosen people. In both cases, the couple respond by preparing a food offering: Abraham sets curds, milk and 'a choice, tender calf' (Genesis 18:7) before his divine guests, while Manoah prepares a young goat and grain offering for his.

In both cases, the messenger explains something of the promised son's mission: Abraham's son is the one with whom God would establish his covenant 'as an everlasting covenant' for his offspring after him, to multiply him greatly and to make him exceedingly fruitful (Genesis 17:2, 6–7); while Manoah's son would 'begin to save Israel from the hand of the Philistines' (Judges 13:5 ESV).

Additionally, Abraham is instructed to name his son Isaac (Genesis 17:19), while Manoah and his wife are instructed that they should not cut their son's hair and that the mother-to-be should not drink any wine or strong drink, and 'eat nothing unclean, for the child shall be a Nazirite to God from the womb to the day of his death' (Judges 13:5, 7 ESV).

The events surrounding the birth of the prophet Samuel echo many of the same features, though with several of the roles reversed. Hannah was the childless wife of a certain man, Elkanah of the tribe of the Ephraimites, because 'the LORD had closed her womb' (1 Samuel 1:5). In this case, Elkanah prepares a meat offering as a sacrifice, but Hannah, like Manoah's angel, abstains from eating it (v. 4). In this case, Hannah takes the initiative in praying for a son. It is also Hannah who outlines both his mission and additional instructions for his life: 'I will give him to the LORD for all the days of his life, and no razor will ever be used on his head' (v. 11). Further, in this case, it is the divine messenger who responds, in the person of Eli the priest, by blessing Hannah: 'may the God of Israel grant you what you have asked of him' (v. 17). In another parallel, later in the story, just as Manoah at first did not recognise that his visitor was in fact the Lord, so too the young boy Samuel initially does not recognise that it is the Lord who is calling him (1 Samuel 3).

Isaiah the prophet later tells the people of Judah:

> The virgin will conceive and give birth to a son, and will call him Immanuel … Before the boy knows enough to reject the wrong and choose the right, the land of the two kings you dread will be laid waste. The LORD will bring on you and on your people and on the house of your father a time unlike any since Ephraim broke away from Judah – he will bring the king of Assyria.
> (Isaiah 7:14–17)

The context makes clear that this miraculous birth had an immediate fulfilment – before the lands of Aram and Israel were laid waste: in 732 BC and 721 BC, respectively. Yet this prophecy was evidently understood also to apply to the Messiah. As Matthew makes clear, 'All this took place to fulfil what the Lord had said through the prophet: "The virgin will conceive and give birth to a son, and they will call him Immanuel" (which means "God with us")' (Matthew 1:22–3).

Thus, the Law of Moses and the Prophets had prepared the people of God – and us – to expect the miraculous birth of a future deliverer, 'that we might live through him' (1 John 4:9). The story of Christmas begins with the curse of sin and death; but it continues with a promise of life.

Pause to ponder

- In what ways do the lives of these three Old Testament deliverers point us forward to the work of Christ?
- In what areas of *your* life would you like to see more of God's promised blessings of deliverance and life in all its fullness?

Day 3
Out of Egypt

Pharaoh gave this order to all his people: 'Every Hebrew boy that is born you must throw into the Nile, but let every girl live.'

Now a man of the tribe of Levi married a Levite woman, and she became pregnant and gave birth to a son. When she saw that he was a fine child, she hid him for three months. But when she could hide him no longer, she got a papyrus basket for him and coated it with tar and pitch. Then she placed the child in it and put it among the reeds along the bank of the Nile. His sister stood at a distance to see what would happen to him.

Then Pharaoh's daughter went down to the Nile to bathe, and her attendants were walking along the river-bank. She saw the basket among the reeds and sent her female slave to get it. She opened it and saw the baby. He was crying, and she felt sorry for him. 'This is one of the Hebrew babies,' she said.

Then his sister asked Pharaoh's daughter, 'Shall I go and get one of the Hebrew women to nurse the baby for you?'

'Yes, go,' she answered. So the girl went and got the baby's mother. Pharaoh's daughter said to her, 'Take this baby and nurse him for me, and I will pay you.' So the woman took the baby and nursed him. When the child grew older, she took him to Pharaoh's daughter and he became her son. She named him Moses, saying, 'I drew him out of the water.'
(Exodus 1:22 – 2:10)

Quick glance

The last fourteen chapters of Genesis recount how God sent Joseph to Egypt ahead of his brothers and parents 'to preserve life'. He and the multitude of other deliverers that appear throughout the history of Israel could only ever preserve life for a brief period. Nevertheless, they pointed the people of God forward to the promised miracle-birth deliverer who would be able to preserve life for ever. The focus for the remaining four books of the Torah – the first five books of the Bible – is Moses. At the time of his birth, he was himself rescued from a massacre of infants. Through Moses, God led his people out of Egypt and established the Book of the Covenant so that they might 'enjoy long life'. As we anticipate celebrating the miraculous birth of the promised deliverer, we can look to Israel's most illustrious deliverer, Moses, to learn more about the promise of life fulfilled in the Messiah.

In-depth reflection

In the beginning, 'the LORD God formed the man of dust from the ground and breathed into his nostrils the breath of life' (Genesis 2:7 ESV). Human beings, however, rejected the good blessings of God, preferring to embrace knowledge of evil. As a consequence, we became subject to the curse, cut off from the tree of life and condemned to return to the dust from which we came (Genesis 3:19, 22–4).

The last fourteen chapters of Genesis – a narrative described as 'the generations of Jacob' (Genesis 37:2 ESV) – recount how God sent Jacob's son Joseph to Egypt ahead of his brothers and parents, in the words of 45:5, 'to preserve life'. He, along with the multitude of other deliverers who appear throughout the history of Israel, could only ever preserve life for a brief period. The curse of death would always prove greater than any temporary relief that these human deliverers could bring. Nevertheless, they highlighted God's desire that we, who were created in his own image, should again ultimately 'have life, and have it to the full' (John 10:10). The story of Joseph thus pointed the people of God forward to the promised miracle-birth deliverer who would be able to preserve life for ever.

After Joseph, the record of God's dealings with his people skips forward several generations to their deliverance from Egypt by Moses. The Lord had revealed to Abraham that 'for four hundred years' his descendants would be 'strangers in a country not their own' and they would be 'enslaved and ill-treated there' (Genesis 15:13). Of this period, we are simply told that the Israelites multiplied greatly but that the Egyptians 'put slave masters over them to oppress them with forced labour' and 'worked them ruthlessly' (Exodus 1:6–14). The focus for the remaining four books of the Torah – the first five books of the Bible – is Moses.

Significantly, the first thing that we learn about Moses, Israel's long-awaited deliverer, is that he himself was preserved from death at the time of his birth. Pharaoh had commanded that all Hebrew boys should be killed. Yet, through the combined actions of the midwives, his mother, his sister, Pharaoh's daughter and her attendants, the future deliverer was preserved (Exodus 2:1–10).

Interestingly, especially in a book with the title (in the original Hebrew) of 'Names' (*Shemot*), among all of these individuals, only the two Hebrew midwives are named: Shiphrah and Puah. The identity of the baby's parents appears to be irrelevant to the story. We are simply told that 'a man of the tribe of Levi married a Levite woman'. Indeed, they are not named until Exodus 6:20, where we are informed that 'Amram married his father's sister Jochebed, who bore him Aaron and Moses' – a marriage that God's people would soon learn, through Moses, was contrary to God's designs (Leviticus 18:12). The baby's sister is not named until Exodus 15:20, and even then she is only identified as 'Miriam the prophet, Aaron's sister'. We have to wait until Numbers 26:59 before she is explicitly referred to as Moses' sister. The names of Pharaoh's daughter and her attendants, along with Pharaoh himself, are not recorded at all. Even the baby himself is not named until the end of the section, after he has been weaned and becomes the son of Pharaoh's daughter. Presumably, the names of Shiphrah and Puah are recorded because 'the midwives … feared God' and 'did not do what the king of Egypt had told them to do' but 'let the boys live' (Exodus 1:17–21).

So Israel's deliverance begins with a baby boy rescued from a massacre of infants who becomes the son of someone not his biological parent. If that sounds somewhat familiar, it is probably supposed to! In parallel circumstances, we know that Herod 'gave orders to kill all the boys in Bethlehem and its vicinity who were two years old and under' (Matthew 2:16). Jesus escaped because an angel of the Lord warned Joseph in a dream to 'take the child and his mother, and flee to Egypt'. Later, after the death of Herod, an angel of the Lord again appeared in a dream to Joseph, saying: 'Rise, take the child and his mother and go to the land of Israel.' Between these two references to Jesus as 'the child' (vv. 13 and 20 ESV), we are told that, 'This was to fulfil what the Lord had spoken by the prophet, "Out of Egypt I called my son"' (Matthew 2:15 ESV). In other words, just as the child Moses became the son of Pharaoh's daughter, the child Jesus is God's Son but, as we saw on the first day of our Advent adventure, he became known as 'the son of Joseph' (John 1:45).

Interestingly, in Hebrews 11, which chronicles the ways in which many biblical characters exercised faith, it is noted: 'By faith Moses, when he was grown up, refused to be called the son of Pharaoh's daughter' (Hebrews 11:24). In a similar way, Jesus, when he was grown up, seemingly refused to be called the son of his earthly mother, Mary. He taught us to cry out to our creator God using the colloquial name *Abba* – that is, 'Dad' – in conjunction with the more formal term 'Father' (Mark 14:36; see also Romans 8:15 and Galatians 4:6).[1] Yet, when Jesus starts performing his signs, during the wedding at Cana in Galilee, he does not call his mother *'Imma'* – that is, 'Mum'. Instead he calls her 'Woman' (John 2:4). Later, when people were saying that he was out of his mind, and he was told that his mother and his brothers had come and were calling him, he 'answered them, "Who are my mother and my brothers?" And looking about at those who sat around him, he said, "Here

---

[1] James Barr, '"Abba" Isn't "Daddy"', *Journal of Theological Studies*, vol. 39, no. 1 (1988), pp. 28–47.

are my mother and my brothers!'" (Mark 3:33–4 ESV). Lastly, as he hung on the cross, he again called his mother 'Woman', telling her and the disciple whom he loved, who were standing nearby, 'Here is your son' and 'Here is your mother', respectively (John 19:26–7).

Coming back to Moses, when the Israelites groaned in their slavery and cried out for help, God remembered his covenant with Abraham, Isaac and Jacob. He revealed himself to the man Moses, whom he had rescued as a baby from destruction (Exodus 3). Through him, God led his people out of Egypt to give them the land he had promised on oath to their ancestors and, in Exodus 24, established the Book of the Covenant so that they might 'enjoy long life' (Deuteronomy 6).

Evidently, if we are to enjoy the life promised in the Christ-child, we should follow the clues that were first revealed centuries earlier. The New Testament was not written until after the death and resurrection of Jesus. Its Gospels and letters help us to understand better why 'the Word became flesh and made his dwelling among us' (John 1:14). Yet we can clearly gain extra insight by trying to imagine what it must have been like for those who witnessed the events of his life first-hand. Unlike us, they did not know about the resurrection and ascension of Jesus and they did not have the New Testament to inform their understanding of his life and mission. The pattern that began with Jacob's son Joseph, of one who would 'preserve life' for the people of God, continues on a grand scale with Moses. As we anticipate celebrating the miraculous birth of the promised deliverer, we too should look to Israel's most illustrious deliverer, Moses, to learn more about the promise of life fulfilled in the Messiah.

Pause to ponder

- What do (or did) you call your father (or father figure)? How comfortable are you in using the same term to address our heavenly Father when you talk to him in prayer?
- What challenge in your family, community or the wider world most causes *you* to cry out to God for help? How might God unexpectedly be 'preserving life' through this situation?

Day 4
The life of the world

The Lord said to Moses, 'I have heard the grumbling of the people of Israel. Say to them, "At twilight you shall eat meat, and in the morning you shall be filled with bread. Then you shall know that I am the Lord your God."'
(Exodus 16:12 ESV)

Quick glance

Jesus often drew upon imagery from the Law of Moses in his teaching of the crowds. For instance, after the occasion when he miraculously fed more than 5,000 people, Jesus explained that 'the bread of God is *he who comes down from heaven and gives life to the world*'. To eat the flesh of Jesus and to drink his blood is, in the words of John 6:35, to *come to him* and to *believe in him*. As we approach Christmas, we can sometimes, like the hungry crowd, have mixed motives when we seek the Christ-child who came down from heaven. We want our fill now, in this physical life, of joy and peace. Daily, we work and strive to achieve success, security and satisfaction in this life. Yet, when we feed on Christ and believe his teaching, then we shall be truly and fully filled – that is, fulfilled: we shall have eternal life and be raised up on the last day.

In-depth reflection

Jesus often explained who he was and the purpose of his life using imagery from the Law of Moses that pointed forward to him. The day after he miraculously fed a crowd of over 5,000 people, a group

The life of the world

of them find him teaching in the synagogue at Capernaum and ask, 'What must we do, to be doing the works of God?' (John 6:28).[1] When Jesus replies that the work of God is to 'believe in him whom he has sent', they demand: 'Then what sign do you do, that we may see and believe you? What work do you perform? Our fathers ate the manna in the wilderness; as it is written, "He gave them bread from heaven to eat"' (John 6:30–1).

They asked for a sign like the one given by Moses to the grumbling Israelites. In reply, Jesus explains to them:

> Truly, truly, I say to you, it was not Moses who gave you the bread from heaven, but my Father gives you the true bread from heaven. For the bread of God is *he who comes down from heaven and gives life to the world* … I am the bread of life; whoever comes to me shall not hunger …
> (John 6:32–5)

As early as this period of rebellion among the people of God in Exodus 16, the preparations were being laid for us to understand that Jesus would 'come down from heaven … [so] that everyone who looks on the Son and believes in him should have eternal life' (John 6:38–40).

Yet, like those who followed Moses into the wilderness, 'the Jews grumbled about him' and said, 'Is not this Jesus, the son of Joseph, whose father and mother we know? How does he now say, "I have come down from heaven"?' (John 6:41–2).

Jesus responds by emphasising the contrast between the former plight of death and the new promise of life: 'Your fathers ate the manna in the wilderness, and they died. This is the bread that comes down from heaven, so that one may eat of it and not die. I am the living bread that came down from heaven.' Seeming to deepen their confusion, he adds: 'If anyone eats of this bread, he will live for ever. And the bread that I will give for the life of the world is my flesh' (6:49–51).

---

[1] All quotations from John chapter 6 in this day's reflection are from ESV.

Day 4

Understandably, just as many of us might still do today, 'the Jews then disputed among themselves, saying, "How can this man give us his flesh to eat?"' Cryptically, Jesus doubles down on his seemingly cannibalistic metaphor, teaching them: 'unless you eat the flesh of the Son of Man and drink his blood, you have no life in you. Whoever feeds on my flesh and drinks my blood has eternal life, and I will raise him up on the last day' (6:52–4).

In case any of his listeners missed what they must do, he stresses again: 'For my flesh is true food, and my blood is true drink. Whoever feeds on my flesh and drinks my blood abides in me, and I in him.' He also repeats that through him life itself, promised for so long, is being made available: 'As the living Father sent me, and I live because of the Father, so whoever feeds on me, he also will live because of me.' Finally, he links this offer of life to their initial demand for a sign like the manna given by Moses: 'This is the bread that came down from heaven, not like the bread the fathers ate and died. Whoever feeds on this bread will live for ever' (6:55–8).

At this point, we need to eavesdrop on a more private conversation that Jesus had with his disciples. The context is similar, in that he had again miraculously fed a large crowd – of 'four thousand men, besides women and children' – and he had just been challenged, this time by the Pharisees and Sadducees, to show them a sign (Matthew 15:38 – 16:1).

Afterwards, Jesus warns the disciples to be on their guard against the yeast of the Pharisees and Sadducees. It is clear that they haven't got a clue what he is talking about. 'Do you still not understand?' he asks them. 'Don't you remember the five loaves for the five thousand, and how many basketfuls you gathered? Or the seven loaves for the four thousand, and how many basketfuls you gathered? How is it you don't understand that I was not talking to you about bread?'

Somehow, this was enough for the penny finally to drop. 'Then they understood that he was not telling them to guard against the yeast used in bread, but against the teaching of the Pharisees and Sadducees' (Matthew 16:5–12).

The life of the world

So, just as Jesus used yeast as a metaphor for the teaching of the Pharisees and Sadducees, in John 6 he uses bread as a metaphor for his own teaching and the substance of what he taught. As the parallel between verses 40 and 54 makes clear (see Table 1), to eat the flesh of Jesus and to drink his blood is to look on the Son and to believe in him – or, in the words of verse 35, to *come to him* and to *believe in him*.

The crowds had seen the previous day that Jesus was able to provide them with sufficient bread to meet their physical needs. Now he was inviting them to recognise that he was equally able to meet their spiritual needs.

Seven times in this passage, we are told that Jesus 'came down from heaven'. Jesus says that he came down from heaven to give 'life to the world' (John 6:33). Four times, he is clear that this means 'eternal life'. Indeed, without him, we 'have no life' in us. As Jesus goes on to explain to the disciples afterwards, 'It is the Spirit who gives life.' To be clear: 'the flesh' (or physical bread and wine) is 'no help at all' (6:63). Without the eternal, spiritual life that becomes ours if we come to and believe in the one who came down from heaven, our lives are nothing – we have no true life at all.

When Jesus began to teach the crowd in the synagogue, he rebuked them: 'You are seeking me, not because you saw signs, but because you ate your fill of the loaves.' As we approach Christmas, we too can seek him with mixed motives. We want our fill now, in this physical life, of joy and peace. Daily, we work and strive to achieve success, security and satisfaction in this life. Yet the child who came down from heaven would urge us with the same appeal he gave the crowds: 'Do not [work] for the food that perishes, but

Table 1 Parallel wording in two sayings of Jesus in John 6

John 6:40 ESV	John 6:54 ESV
Everyone who <u>looks</u> on the Son and <u>believes</u> in him should have *eternal life*, **and I will raise him up on the last day.**	Whoever <u>feeds</u> on my flesh and <u>drinks</u> my blood has *eternal life*, **and I will raise him up on the last day.**

for the food that endures to eternal life, which the Son of Man will give to you' (John 6:26–7).

When we come to the Christ-child and believe in him, as God told the grumbling Israelites through Moses: 'Then you shall know that I am the LORD your God.' More than that, when we feed on and believe his teaching, then we shall be truly and fully filled – that is, fulfilled: we shall have eternal life and be raised up on the last day. For, as an adult, Christ gave his flesh for the life of the world.

Pause to ponder

- To what extent would you claim to have experience of 'the Spirit who gives life'? What do you think greater fullness of this life of the Spirit could look like?
- What would you describe as *your* biggest need? In what ways might Christ satisfy that need as you feed on him and his teaching?

Day 5
The Christmas donkey

The prophecy of Balaam son of Beor,
    the prophecy of one whose eye sees clearly,
the prophecy of one who hears the words of God,
    who has knowledge from the Most High,
who sees a vision from the Almighty,
    who falls prostrate, and whose eyes are opened:

'I see him, but not now;
    I behold him, but not near.
A star will come out of Jacob;
    a sceptre will rise out of Israel.
He will crush the foreheads of Moab,
    the skulls of all the people of Sheth.
Edom will be conquered;
    Seir, his enemy, will be conquered,
    but Israel will grow strong.
A ruler will come out of Jacob
    and destroy the survivors of the city.'
(Numbers 24:15–19)

Quick glance

There are three donkeys associated in the Bible with Jesus. Contrary to our traditional nativity scenes, none of them is connected with Joseph and Mary or their journey to Bethlehem. Two of them are associated with Jesus at the end of his earthly life. Only Balaam's donkey has any connection with Jesus' birth. For it bore the messenger who foretold, for an eastern king, that a star – or heavenly king – would one day rise out of Israel and conquer all the peoples of the world. This prophecy may have helped to inform the magi who, centuries later, came from the east to worship the king of the Jews at his birth after they saw his star rise. Either way, the Law and the Prophets are preparing us: our life-giving deliverer from death is none other than the King of kings who will judge the nations.

In-depth reflection

Contrary to our traditional nativity scenes, the Bible makes no mention of a donkey in connection with Joseph and Mary or their journey to Bethlehem. There are, however, three donkeys associated in the Bible with Jesus. Of these, only one is actually mentioned in the New Testament.

The first appears at the end of the first book of the Law, Genesis, when Jacob gathers his sons around him to tell them what will happen to them in days to come:

> [10] The sceptre will not depart from Judah,
>   nor the ruler's staff from between his feet,
> until he to whom it belongs shall come
>   and the obedience of the nations shall be his.
> [11] He will tether his donkey to a vine,
>   his colt to the choicest branch;
> he will wash his garments in wine,
>   his robes in the blood of grapes.
> (Genesis 49:10–11)

It is clear that the first of these two verses refers to the promised Messiah, the ruler of the nations. The second can appear somewhat cryptic until we notice how the image is used elsewhere in Scripture. Isaiah describes someone 'striding forward in the greatness of his strength' (NIV) and 'speaking in righteousness, mighty to save' (ESV), looking splendid in 'garments stained crimson ... like those of one treading the winepress' (Isaiah 63:1–2). This character declares:

> I have trodden the wine press alone,
>   and from the peoples no one was with me;
> I trod them in my anger
>   and trampled them in my wrath;
> their lifeblood spattered on my garments,
>   and stained all my apparel.
> For the day of vengeance was in my heart,
>   and my year of redemption had come.
> (Isaiah 63:3–4 ESV)

Evidently, washing one's garments in the blood of grapes is a biblical idiom for judgement and wrath. The same imagery is used in Revelation, where 'the angel swung his sickle on the earth, gathered its grapes and threw them into the great winepress of God's wrath. They were trampled in the winepress outside the city, and blood flowed out of the press' (Revelation 14:19–20). Later, the author, John, used similar language to describe another scene:

> I saw heaven standing open and there before me was a white horse, whose rider is called Faithful and True. With justice he judges and wages war ... He is dressed in a robe dipped in blood, and his name is the Word of God ... Coming out of his mouth is a sharp sword with which to strike down the nations. 'He will rule them with an iron sceptre.' He treads the winepress of the fury of the wrath of God Almighty.
> (Revelation 19:11–15)

Yet, in the midst of this judgement, observe also the notes of redemption. The righteous one whose garments were spattered crimson was 'mighty to save' and his 'year of redemption had come'. As Isaiah continues: 'My own arm brought me salvation' (Isaiah 63:5 ESV).

This picture of a righteous, victorious ruler is to be found in connection with another of the donkeys associated with Jesus, this time in the Prophets:

Day 5

> Rejoice greatly, Daughter Zion!
>   Shout, Daughter Jerusalem!
> See, your king comes to you,
>   righteous and victorious,
> lowly and riding on a donkey,
>   on a colt, the foal of a donkey.
> (Zechariah 9:9)

Here, though, there is a key difference. In Isaiah, the blood mentioned was the lifeblood of the objects of God's wrath. In Zechariah, it is 'the blood of my covenant with you' (v. 11), by which God will free Jerusalem's prisoners.

It is therefore unsurprising that two of the Gospel writers cited this passage as coming to pass towards the end of Jesus' earthly life (Matthew 21:1–7; John 12:14–16). The timing was when Jesus approached Jerusalem, ahead of 'his departure [literally, exodus], which he was about to bring to fulfilment at Jerusalem' (Luke 9:31) through the spilling of his own blood.

Thus, the donkeys of both Genesis 49 and Zechariah 9 are associated with Jesus at the end of his life.

Only the third donkey associated with Jesus has any connection with his birth – namely, Balaam's donkey: '[Balaam son of Bezer] was rebuked for his wrongdoing by a donkey – an animal without speech – who spoke with a human voice and restrained the prophet's madness' (2 Peter 2:16).

The account of how God reproached this practitioner of divination through his donkey is recorded in Numbers 22. In this passage, the king of one of Israel's neighbours, Balak, had summoned Balaam to curse the people of God. The Lord's angel had come out against Balaam 'as an adversary' or, literally, 'as Satan' (see vv. 22 and 32) – the first occurrences of this word in the Bible[1] – 'because', he said, 'the journey is impetuous to me' (literal translation). Elsewhere, the Bible and other historical sources indicate

---

[1] See 1 Samuel 29:4 and 2 Samuel 19:22 for examples of situations where the 'adversary' is clearly a person.

that Balaam 'practised divination' (Numbers 22:7; 23:23; Joshua 13:22 ESV), 'loved the wages of wickedness' (2 Peter 2:15; Jude 11), 'taught Balak to entice the Israelites to sin' (Revelation 2:14) and looked to other gods besides the Lord.[2]

An interesting fact typically overlooked is that the word translated 'donkey' and its associated verbs make explicit that Balaam's donkey is female. After Balaam repeatedly beats her and scolds her, she could have rebuked him: 'If you weren't so abusive and such a spiritually blind "seer", you would see that I am protecting you.' Instead, with grace, the she-donkey gently asks Balaam three questions that invite him to reflect truthfully on his road rage, their relationship and her faithful service. The contrast with the other animal that speaks in the Old Testament Law (whom we encountered on day 1) – namely, the serpent, who *is* Satan and who deceitfully addresses the first woman – could not be greater. In both accounts, eyes are opened (Genesis 3:7; Numbers 22:31), but in one a blessing is consequently turned to a curse, while in the other a curse is turned to a blessing (Genesis 3:14–23; Numbers 23:11; 24:10).

For our purposes, however, the important thing is not the miracle of God speaking through an animal. Our attention should instead be on the words of prophecy that God subsequently gives to Balaam: 'A star will come out of Jacob; a sceptre will rise out of Israel.' As with many words of prophecy, this appears to have in mind both an initial and an ultimate fulfilment. The initial fulfilment comes with the rise of King David, who is said to have conquered his enemies Moab, Edom and Seir (2 Samuel 8:1–12; 1 Chronicles 18:1–13). A later initial fulfilment comes in the time of Jehoshaphat, king of Judah, who defeated the inhabitants of Ammon, Moab and Mount Seir (2 Chronicles 20:22–3).

Balaam's reference to 'all the people of Sheth' is interesting, as this particular people is not mentioned anywhere else. 'Sheth' is

---

2 'Deir 'Alla Inscription', Livius (no date): https://www.livius.org/sources/content/deir-alla-inscription (accessed 1 December 2023).

Day 5

the same word elsewhere translated 'Seth', the son born to Adam and Eve after Cain killed Abel. So it would seem to be fairly all-encompassing and suggestive of an ultimate fulfilment beyond any of the Old Testament kings of Judah.

In addition, the description of the ruler who will come out of Jacob – or, more precisely, the 'one from Jacob' who 'shall exercise *dominion*' – uses a word that elsewhere occurs only in Psalm 72. This psalm of Solomon looks forward to the king whose *dominion* will stretch 'from sea to sea, and from the River to the ends of the earth' (v. 8 ESV). It anticipates a king to whom the kings of distant shores will bring tribute and present gifts. It describes a king to whom all kings will bow down and whom all nations will serve. This is clearly the King of kings.

This identification is supported by the parallel image in Balaam's next line – of a sceptre that will rise out of Israel. This links the star to the words of Jacob that we noted above in Genesis 49. The star is the same as the sceptre to whom belongs 'the obedience of the nations' – which is partly why, at the very end of the Bible, we find that Jesus is called the 'bright Morning Star' (Revelation 22:16).

Thus, the sole donkey associated with the account of Jesus' birth was the one through which the Lord miraculously spoke to his prophet Balaam. This donkey did not bear the mother of Jesus. Instead, it bore the messenger who foretold, for an eastern king, that a star – or heavenly king – would one day ('but not now') rise out of Israel and conquer all the descendants of Seth.

Could it be that this prophecy of Balaam helped to inform the magi who, centuries later, came from the east to worship the king of the Jews at his birth after they saw his star rise? According to the chief priests and teachers of the law, this ruler is the same as the one that Micah said would come out of Bethlehem to 'shepherd my people Israel' (Matthew 2:1–12). Either way, the Law and the Prophets are preparing us: our life-giving deliverer from death is none other than the King of kings who will judge the nations.

Pause to ponder

- In what areas of your life do you most resist the dominion of the King of kings? How might you surrender more fully to Christ as Lord in the year ahead?
- What lessons might we draw by contrasting the conversations of Balaam and Eve with speaking animals? In what ways might these help us to understand the appearances of angels and Satan in the Gospels?

Day 6
A prophet like Moses

The LORD your God will raise up for you a prophet like me from among you, from your fellow Israelites. You must listen to him. For this is what you asked of the LORD your God at Horeb on the day of the assembly when you said, 'Let us not hear the voice of the LORD our God nor see this great fire any more, or we will die.'

The LORD said to me: 'What they say is good. I will raise up for them a prophet like you from among their fellow Israelites, and I will put my words in his mouth. He will tell them everything I command him. I myself will call to account anyone who does not listen to my words that the prophet speaks in my name.'
(Deuteronomy 18:15–19)

Quick glance

The Law unexpectedly includes a promise that the Lord would raise up a prophet like Moses from among the Israelites. This clearly refers to the promised deliverer who would bring life, and the early church applied this promise to 'the Messiah, who has been appointed for you – even Jesus'. It reveals three key things about Jesus. First, the Lord would put his words in Jesus' mouth. Second, Jesus would tell the people everything the Lord commanded him. Third, the Lord himself will call to account anyone who does not listen to his words that the prophet speaks in his name. In fact, Jesus himself will call us all to account, for 'the Father judges no one, but has entrusted all judgment to the Son'. So the helpless figure that we behold in the Christmas manger is the long-awaited

'Prophet like Moses' to whom we are told we must listen, for he is the King of kings who will judge the nations.

In-depth reflection

Before we move on from the Law of Moses in our quest for insights into the baby of Bethlehem, we should consider the passage above. In a section warning against listening to those who practise sorcery or divination, the Law unexpectedly includes this promise that the Lord would raise up a prophet like Moses from among the Israelites.

We might think that this would be Moses' successor, Joshua son of Nun. When Moses died, in Moab, we are told that Joshua 'was filled with the spirit of wisdom' and that 'the Israelites listened to him and did what the LORD had commanded Moses' (Deuteronomy 34:9). So we might suppose that the promise in chapter 18 simply refers to Joshua.

This would, however, be a strangely transient item to include in the middle of a long list of enduring guidance intended to show future generations of God's people how they should best conduct their lives. Moreover, the passage about Joshua immediately continues:

> Since then, no prophet has risen in Israel like Moses, whom the LORD knew face to face, who did all those signs and wonders the LORD sent him to do in Egypt – to Pharaoh and to all his officials and to his whole land. For no one has ever shown the mighty power or performed the awesome deeds that Moses did in the sight of all Israel.
> (Deuteronomy 34:10–12)

So, although Joshua 'was filled with the spirit of wisdom', neither he nor any of his successors was a prophet 'like Moses, whom the LORD knew face to face'. No other prophet 'has ever shown the mighty power or performed the awesome deeds that Moses did'.

It is clear, then, that the promise that God would raise up a prophet like Moses refers uniquely to the promised deliverer who

Day 6

would bring life. In the early days of the Church, Peter indeed applied this promise to 'the Messiah, who has been appointed for you – even Jesus' (Acts 3:20–2). We have already observed (on day 3) parallels between the birth narratives of Moses and Jesus. We also saw (on day 4) how Jesus claimed he could meet our needs more deeply than Moses did. Furthermore, although Moses was never called a king (Deuteronomy 33:5 most probably refers to the Lord), he was certainly the deliverer, shepherd and judge of Israel.

Here, then, in the middle of the decrees and laws given to God's people through Moses, we are told three key things about Jesus. First, the Lord would put his words in his mouth. Jesus often instructed the crowds that came to him to listen. More specifically, he told them to 'consider carefully how you listen' and to 'listen and understand' (Luke 8:18; Matthew 15:10). He concluded his famous lesson on the mountain with the following words:

> Everyone who hears these words of mine and puts them into practice is like a wise man who built his house on the rock. The rain came down, the streams rose, and the winds blew and beat against that house; yet it did not fall, because it had its foundation on the rock. But everyone who hears these words of mine and does not put them into practice is like a foolish man who built his house on sand. The rain came down, the streams rose, and the winds blew and beat against that house, and it fell with a great crash.
> (Matthew 7:24–7)

The Lord put his words in the mouth of Jesus, the Prophet like Moses. So we would be wise to heed them and to put them into practice.

Second, Jesus would tell the people everything the Lord commanded him. He withheld nothing of the words that the Lord put in his mouth. On one occasion, Jesus said: 'he who sent me is trustworthy, and what I have heard from him I tell the world ... I do nothing on my own but speak just what the Father has taught me' (John 8:26, 28). We noted yesterday that the name of the righteous judge is 'the Word of God' (Revelation 19:13). This picks up the language with which John begins his Gospel account:

> In the beginning was the Word, and the Word was with God, and the Word was God. He was with God in the beginning. Through him all things were made; without him nothing was made that has been made ... The Word became flesh and made his dwelling among us.
> (John 1:1–3, 14)

The Lord put his words in the mouth of Jesus, the Prophet like Moses, and he in turn told the people everything the Lord commanded him. For the long-awaited deliverer was none other than the Word of God.

Third, the Lord himself will call to account anyone who does not listen to his words that the prophet speaks in his name. In fact, it is Jesus himself who will call us all to account: 'The Father judges no one, but has entrusted all judgment to the Son ... And [the Father] has given him authority to judge because he is the Son of Man' (John 5:22, 27). Jesus' disciple John also testified about him:

> The one who comes from heaven is above all. He testifies to what he has seen and heard, but no one accepts his testimony. Whoever has accepted it has certified that God is truthful. For the one whom God has sent speaks the words of God, for God gives the Spirit without limit. The Father loves the Son and has placed everything in his hands. Whoever believes in the Son has eternal life, but whoever rejects the Son will not see life, for God's wrath remains on them.
> (John 3:31–6)

We saw (on day 4) that Jesus identified himself as the one who came from heaven. Here John makes much the same three points about him that the Law revealed about the future Prophet like Moses: first, he testifies to what he has heard; second, he speaks the words of God; and third, God's wrath remains on whoever rejects the Son – the one sent by God into the world to save the world (John 3:17). So we see that the long-awaited Prophet like Moses is the Lord himself – the Lord incarnate. The helpless figure that we behold in the Christmas manger is the one to whom we are told we must listen, for he is the King of kings who will judge the nations.

Pause to ponder

- How many key ways can you think of in which Jesus was 'a prophet like Moses'? In what ways was he greater than Moses in his likeness?
- Which sayings of Jesus do you find most difficult to *heed*? How might you become more attentive to his inspired words in the coming year?

Day 7
The Nazirite

The angel of the LORD appeared to the woman and said to her, 'Behold, you are barren and have not borne children, but you shall conceive and bear a son. Therefore be careful and drink no wine or strong drink, and eat nothing unclean, for behold, you shall conceive and bear a son. No razor shall come upon his head, for the child shall be a Nazirite to God from the womb, and he shall begin to save Israel from the hand of the Philistines.'
(Judges 13:3–5 ESV)

Quick glance

When the angel revealed to Manoah the Danite and his barren wife that she would bear a son who would 'begin to save Israel from the hand of the Philistines', they were charged not to cut their son's hair and she was instructed to abstain from certain food and drink. This was because 'the child [would] be a *Nazirite* to God from the womb'. Elsewhere, this Hebrew word clearly means something or someone separated for a special purpose. God had called Israel to be a people separate among the nations in order to become a blessing to all the peoples of the world. Instead, it embraced the ways of the nations and became 'a curse among the nations'. In contrast, Jesus is the *Separated One* who would save God's people and through whom 'all nations on earth [would] be blessed'. Whereas the earlier deliverers, such as Samson, would 'begin to save God's people', Jesus came down from heaven and was '*separated* to God' to complete our salvation – to save us once and for all.

In-depth reflection

Earlier in our reflections (on day 2) we saw that the Law and the Prophets prepare us for the miraculous birth of a future deliverer foretold by divine messengers. In the context of the promises made to Abraham and Sarah, we noted some of the elements that recur in subsequent miraculous births leading up to that of Jesus.

Beginning with the judge Samson, we observed that an angel appeared to the wife of a certain man, Manoah of the tribe of the Danites, who was barren and had borne no children. Promising that she would conceive and bear a son, the divine messenger revealed that the son would 'begin to save Israel from the hand of the Philistines' (Judges 13:5).

Evidently, Manoah's wife has both greater spiritual discernment and greater faith than her husband. She immediately tells him, 'A man of God came to me. He looked like an angel of God, very awesome.' Note how she adds, 'I didn't ask him where he came from, and he didn't tell me his name' (v. 6).

Understandably, Manoah appears to be somewhat sceptical. So he prays to the Lord: 'Pardon your servant, Lord. I beg you to let the man of God you sent to us come again to teach us how to bring up the boy who is to be born' (Judges 13:8). In his mercy, God sends his messenger again. Speaking this time with Manoah, the angel repeats what he previously told the woman. In this we can see a parallel with the events leading up to the birth of Jesus. For the angel of the Lord that appeared to Joseph in a dream provided personal reassurance but added nothing to what had already been revealed to Mary (Matthew 1:20–1; compare Luke 1:26–38).

Manoah apparently believes that the messenger is simply a holy man, for he asks, 'What is your name, so that we may honour you when your word comes true?' Only after the angel later departs does Manoah realise that it was the angel of the Lord. At this point, somewhat melodramatically, he laments: 'We are doomed to die! … We have seen God!' (Judges 13:22).

His wife, with deeper insight and faith, more sensibly reassures him: 'If the Lord had meant to kill us, he would not have accepted a burnt offering and grain offering from our hands, nor shown us all these things or now told us this' (v. 23).

Before departing, the angel responds to Manoah's question with the words, 'Why do you ask my name, seeing it is wonderful?' (v. 18 ESV). The Hebrew word for 'wonderful' means 'incomprehensible'. It occurs in the same form in just one other place in the Old Testament – in Psalm 139:6 (ESV): 'Such knowledge is too wonderful for me; it is high; I cannot attain it.' A different form of the word features in a passage that is so familiar to many of us that we are unable to read it without hearing the Christmas music of Handel's *Messiah*:

> For to us a child is born,
>   to us a son is given;
> and the government shall be upon his shoulder,
>   and his name shall be called
> *Wonderful* Counsellor, Mighty God,
>   Everlasting Father, Prince of Peace.
> (Isaiah 9:6 ESV)

It is almost incomprehensible to us when we consider that the name of the angel of the Lord was too wonderful for Manoah and his wife to hear, yet to us a child has been born whose name has been revealed to be Jesus — 'Son of the Most High', 'the Word of God', and 'King of kings and Lord of lords' (Luke 1:32; Revelation 19:13, 16).

Unlike Abraham and Sarah – or Joseph and Mary – Manoah and his wife are not instructed about what to call their son. Instead, they are charged not to cut their son's hair and told that she should eat nothing unclean and abstain from wine and strong drink. The reason given for this is that 'the child shall be a *Nazirite* to God from the womb'.

Our word *Nazirite* is from a Hebrew word that in three Bible passages is transliterated into English, rather than being translated. Besides here in Judges 13, the other two passages are Numbers 6, which sets out what someone should do who 'wants to make

Day 7

a special vow, a vow of dedication to the LORD' (v. 2), and Amos 2:11–12, in which the Lord refers to raising up Nazirites in the same way that he raises up prophets. Elsewhere, the word clearly means something or someone separated for a special purpose. So, when Jacob prophesies over his sons, he concludes his blessing of Joseph with the words 'Let all these rest on the head of Joseph, on the brow of the *one separated from* his brothers' (Genesis 49:26, alternative translation). As we have already noted, Joseph was *separated from* his family to preserve the life of God's people. In the laws concerning the Sabbath year and Jubilee year, God's people are instructed not to reap what grows of itself or to harvest (literally) 'the *separated* (or consecrated) grapes' (Leviticus 25:5, 11).

The related Hebrew word *nazar* is used in a similar way. For example, God tells Moses: '*keep* the Israelites *separate from* things that make them unclean' (Leviticus 15:31) and 'Tell Aaron and his sons to *keep separate from* the sacred offerings the Israelites consecrate to me, so they will not profane my holy name' (Leviticus 22:2, literal translation). In this verse, we see that it has a parallel sense to the Hebrew root translated variously as 'sacred', 'consecrated' and 'holy'. In contrast, the prophets also talk of those who *separate themselves from* the Lord (Ezekiel 14:7) and who *separate themselves to* idols (Hosea 9:10).

So, Manoah and his wife were divinely instructed that their child should be *separated* to God 'from the womb'. The question is: as we gaze on the infant Jesus and see in him the fulfilment of the historic pattern of miraculously born deliverers, what are we to make of this instruction about Samson?

We saw earlier how God repeatedly promised Abraham that through him 'all peoples on earth [would] be blessed' and that through his offspring 'all nations on earth [would] be blessed' (Genesis 12:3; 22:18). This promise was reaffirmed to his son Isaac in exactly the same words (Genesis 26:4). God had called Israel to be a people separate among the nations. As he instructed Moses to tell the people of Israel: 'out of all nations you will be my treasured possession. Although the whole earth is mine, you will be for me a kingdom of priests and a holy nation' (Exodus 19:5–6). The people of Israel were to be holy – that is, set apart or separated from the other nations – in order to become a blessing to all the peoples of the world.

So, too, the birth of Jesus is significant because he was '*separated to God from the womb to the day of his death*' (Judges 13:7) in order to become a blessing to all the peoples of the world. Israel as a nation had repeatedly fallen short of its calling. It had embraced the ways of the nations, instead of being separate from them. As a consequence, instead of being a blessing, it became 'a curse among the nations' (Zechariah 8:13; also Jeremiah 29:18; 44:8). In contrast, Jesus is the *Separated One*, who would save God's people and through whom 'all nations on earth [would] be blessed'.

Intriguingly, Matthew seems to point to this when he tells us about the first years of Jesus' life:

> [Joseph] took the child and his mother and went to the land of Israel. But when he heard that Archelaus was reigning in Judea in place of his father Herod, he was afraid to go there. Having been warned in a dream, he withdrew to the district of Galilee, and he went and lived in a town called Nazareth. So was fulfilled what was said through the prophets, that he would be called a Nazarene.
> (Matthew 2:21–3)

The Greek word most frequently translated as 'Nazarene' in the New Testament is *nazōraios* (fifteen times). This is different from that used elsewhere to signify a person from Nazareth, namely *nazarēnos* (four times). With the exception of Matthew 2:23, on all but one occasion out of the fifteen times *nazōraios* is used in the New Testament, it is alongside the name Jesus. The only other instance is when Paul is accused of being 'a ringleader of the Nazarene sect' (Acts 24:5). This could, plausibly, be translated 'the sect of the Separated Ones' – or 'sect of the Nazirites'. In which case, when used to describe Jesus, it should perhaps be read as a title, in the same way that we use the word *Christ*, which means 'the Anointed One'.

Day 7

It is important to recognise that, to some extent, the two Greek words are used interchangeably. For instance, during Jesus' trial, when Peter is standing in the courtyard of the high priest and a servant girl accuses Peter of having been with Jesus, Matthew's account uses the word *nazōraios* (26:71), whereas Mark's uses *nazarēnos* (14:67). Nevertheless, there may well be a deliberate ambiguity in the choice of word.

Elsewhere, Matthew exercises a degree of poetic licence when applying other Old Testament quotations to the events of Jesus' birth. For instance, a couple of verses earlier in chapter 2, he quotes a passage from Jeremiah, a description of mourning from the time when Israel was taken into exile, and applies it to Herod's execution of infants in Bethlehem after Jesus is born (Matthew 2:17–18). He next informs us that Joseph took the child Jesus and his mother and 'lived in a town called Nazareth. So was fulfilled what was said through the prophets, that he would be called a [*nazōraios*]' (v. 23). Given that there is no other prophecy recorded for us in Scripture that says the Messiah would be called a *Nazarene*, Matthew probably intended us to understand the deliberate double meaning that Jesus would be called a *Nazirite*. If so, this would underscore how Jesus was the true *Separated One*.

Either way, we see that the newborn Jesus, like Samson, would be *separated* to God 'from the womb to the day of his death'. Whereas the deliverers who came before him, such as Samson, would 'begin to save God's people', Jesus came down from heaven and was '*separated* to God' to complete our salvation – to save us once and for all.

Pause to ponder

- What implications does viewing Jesus as the Separated One have for *your understanding* of the uniqueness of his birth and the purpose for which he was born?
- What implications does it have for *your understanding* of the new life promised to followers of Jesus?

Day 8
Reversal of fortunes

Hannah prayed and said:

'My heart rejoices in the LORD;
　　in the LORD my horn is lifted high.
My mouth boasts over my enemies,
　　for I delight in your deliverance.

'There is no one holy like the LORD;
　　there is no one besides you;
　　there is no Rock like our God.

'Do not keep talking so proudly
　　or let your mouth speak such arrogance,
for the LORD is a God who knows,
　　and by him deeds are weighed.

'The bows of the warriors are broken,
　　but those who stumbled are armed with strength.
Those who were full hire themselves out for food,
　　but those who were hungry are hungry no more.
She who was barren has borne seven children,
　　but she who has had many sons pines away.

'The LORD brings death and makes alive;
　　he brings down to the grave and raises up.
The LORD sends poverty and wealth;
　　he humbles and he exalts.
He raises the poor from the dust

Day 8

> and lifts the needy from the ash heap;
> he seats them with princes
>   and has them inherit a throne of honour.
>
> 'For the foundations of the earth are the LORD's;
>   on them he has set the world.
> He will guard the feet of his faithful servants,
>   but the wicked will be silenced in the place of darkness.
>
> 'It is not by strength that one prevails;
>   those who oppose the LORD will be broken.
> The Most High will thunder from heaven;
>   the LORD will judge the ends of the earth.
>
> 'He will give strength to his king
> and exalt the horn of his anointed.'
> (1 Samuel 2:1–10)

Quick glance

After Samuel the prophet is born, his mother Hannah prays: 'My heart rejoices in the Lord!' Many generations later, her prayer becomes the inspiration for the words of Jesus' mother that are often known as the Magnificat. So Hannah's language gives us insights into Mary's boy child. Both sons were a blessing to their mothers but later became greater blessings to the whole of God's people as deliverers. Hannah's set of contrasting 'reversal of fortunes' emphasises God's sovereign control of all things. She appears to conclude by speaking of the King of kings and Anointed One. Through the Messiah, she signals, the Lord will 'bring death' and 'raise up' from the grave. Through him, the self-reliant will be humbled and the needy will be exalted in honour. So, as we look ahead to the birth of Jesus, Hannah encourages us to anticipate the King who would, in the words of the King James and English Standard versions of the Bible, 'turn the world upside down'.

In-depth reflection

The next stop on our journey towards Bethlehem is the birth of the prophet Samuel. We have already seen (on day 2) that his mother Hannah was childless because 'the LORD had closed her womb' (1 Samuel 1:5). Like Manoah's wife, she demonstrates clear faith in God. Hannah even takes the initiative in praying for a son, and promises to 'give him to the LORD for all the days of his life' (v. 11). In turn, she is blessed by her divine messenger, Eli the priest.

Once Samuel is born and weaned, Hannah takes him to serve in the Temple, where she prays, 'My heart rejoices in the Lord!' Centuries afterwards, Hannah's prayer is evidently drawn upon as inspiration by Jesus' mother Mary when she visits her relative Elizabeth, the mother of John the Baptiser (Luke 1:46–55). In much of its language, Mary's response (often known as the Magnificat) echoes Hannah's prayer. What, then, does Hannah's prayer reveal about Mary's boy child?

First, Hannah's son was initially a blessing for her, but later he became a greater blessing to the whole of God's people as a deliverer. So too with Mary's son. Both mothers begin with a word of individual praise (see Table 2).

While Hannah next says her mouth 'is enlarged over her enemies' (literal translation), Mary's next choice of phrase (see Table 3) recalls the words of another Old Testament mother, Leah, after her servant Zilpah bore Jacob a second son: 'How happy I am! The women will call me happy' (Genesis 30:13). The word here translated 'happy' is more typically rendered 'blessed'. For example, in Psalm 72:17 it follows another common word meaning the same thing: 'all nations will be blessed through him, and they will call him *blessed*'.

Table 2 A word of praise from two mothers of miracle-born sons

Hannah (1 Samuel 2:1)	Mary (Luke 1:46–8)
My heart rejoices in the LORD;	My soul glorifies the Lord and my spirit rejoices in God my Saviour,
in the LORD my horn is lifted high.	for he has been mindful of the humble state of his servant.

Day 8

Table 3 Expressions of delight and blessedness from two mothers

Hannah (1 Samuel 2:1)	Mary (Luke 1:48–9)
My mouth boasts over my enemies, for I delight in your deliverance.	From now on all generations will call me blessed, for the Mighty One has done great things for me …

Both mothers then frame their personal praise within the wider context of what God has done for all his people (see Table 4). They recognise in their own circumstances grounds for praise by the whole community of God's people. Their example should remind us that, whenever we too glorify God – or, better, 'magnify' him or, more literally, 'make him mega' – we should look to see how our individual causes for praise fit into God's grander scheme for all his people. Only then do we see the true cause for praise in all the 'mega things' (literal translation of 'great things') God has done for us. With eyes of faith, Hannah and Mary acknowledge that God has greater purposes for their miracle-born sons.

Table 4 Praise to God for his greater purposes

Hannah (1 Samuel 2:2–5)	Mary (Luke 1:49–53)
There is no one holy like the LORD; there is no one besides you; there is no Rock like our God.	… holy is his name. His mercy extends to those who fear him, from generation to generation.
Do not keep talking so proudly or let your mouth speak such arrogance,	He has performed mighty deeds with his arm;
For the LORD is a God who knows, and by him deeds are weighed.	He has scattered those who are proud in their inmost thoughts.
The bows of the warriors are broken, but those who stumbled are armed with strength.	He has brought down rulers from their thrones but has lifted up the humble.
Those who were full hire themselves out for food, but those who were hungry are hungry no more.	He has filled the hungry with good things but has sent the rich away empty.

Mary closes with the words:

> He has helped his servant Israel,
>   remembering to be merciful
> to Abraham and his descendants for ever,
>   just as he promised our ancestors.
> (Luke 1:54–5)

Significantly, this statement roots the gospel message – even that presented by Luke, whose account is often considered the 'Gospel written for the Gentiles' – firmly in the heritage of Israel. We can only rightly understand Jesus as the fulfilment of the promises of the Law and the Prophets. The mercy that God has shown us is the mercy promised to his servant Israel, in which we now share.

In contrast to Mary, Hannah's prayer continues and is not even halfway finished here. Although Jesus is still within her womb, Mary's response can be read as a declaration that God's promised work has now reached its conclusion – certainly that his promises to Abraham have now been fulfilled. In contrast, Hannah – whose son had already been born and had begun to serve in the Temple – goes on to speak in language that goes beyond God's dealings with just his chosen people.

Initially, Hannah continues the 'reversal of fortunes' theme that she has already expressed, contrasting warriors with those who stumble, the arrogant with the all-knowing God, and the full with the hungry. 'She who was barren has borne seven children, but she who has had many sons pines away' (v. 5). Given that she has only just had one son at this point – and is recorded as later having three sons and two daughters (1 Samuel 2:21) – she is clearly not making a literal reference to herself. Neither is she speaking of Abraham's wife Sarah, for she only had one son, Isaac. So she is probably speaking figuratively, as the number seven is often used in Scripture as the number of perfection or completeness. Yet, as we think about Christmas, it is worth noting that Mary had at least seven children: Jesus, James, Joseph, Judas, Simon and at least two sisters (Mark 6:3). Inspired by God, perhaps Hannah speaks of more than she realises.

Day 8

Hannah then continues her set of contrasting 'reversal of fortunes', emphasising God's sovereign control of all things:

> The LORD brings death and makes alive;
>   he brings down to the grave and raises up.
> The LORD sends poverty and wealth;
>   he humbles and he exalts.
> He raises the poor from the dust
>   and lifts the needy from the ash heap;
> he seats them with princes
>   and has them inherit a throne of honour.
> (1 Samuel 2:6–8)

Rightly do the prophets observe, 'When disaster comes to a city, has not the LORD caused it?' (Amos 3:6). For 'who can speak and have it happen if the Lord has not decreed it? Is it not from the mouth of the Most High that both calamities and good things come?' (Lamentations 3:37–8).

Hannah's prayer then reaches its climax, in which she appears to see things from a heavenly perspective, from outside of space and time:

> For the foundations of the earth are the LORD's;
>   on them he has set the world.
> He will guard the feet of his faithful servants,
>   but the wicked will be silenced in the place of darkness.
>
> It is not by strength that one prevails;
>   those who oppose the LORD will be broken.
> The Most High will thunder from heaven;
>   the LORD will judge the ends of the earth.
>
> He will give strength to his king
>   and exalt the horn of his anointed.
> (1 Samuel 2:8–10)

At this time, Israel did not have a human king. Only when Hannah's son was an old man would the people demand one, and it was her son Samuel who would anoint their first ruler, Saul (1 Samuel 8:5; 10:1). So, since the context in Hannah's prayer is the Lord's creation of the earth and his judgement of the earth – the beginning and end of time – Hannah surely speaks of the King of kings, the Anointed One. Indeed, the word with which she ends her prayer is 'Messiah'.

We saw (on days 5 and 6) how Scripture has already tried to show us that the Anointed King will judge the nations. Hannah now indicates that this Messiah is also connected with the Lord's plans to reverse the fortunes of all. Through the Messiah, she signals, the Lord will 'bring death' and 'raise up' from the grave. Through him, the self-reliant will be humbled and the needy will be exalted in honour.

Luke too goes on to draw out some of these connections in his Gospel account. For instance, following Mary's response to Elizabeth, Luke records the first words of John the Baptiser's father, Zechariah, after the birth of John. Zechariah's worship begins and ends with allusions to the horn of the anointed, the feet of God's servants, and the place of darkness from Hannah's prayer:

> Praise be to the Lord, the God of Israel,
>   because he has come to his people and redeemed them.
> He has raised up a horn of salvation for us
>   in the house of his servant David …
> because of the tender mercy of our God,
>   by which the rising sun will come to us from heaven
> to shine on those living in darkness
>   and in the shadow of death,
> to guide our feet into the path of peace.
> (Luke 1:68–79)

So, as we look ahead to the birth of Jesus, Hannah encourages us to anticipate the King of whom it is written, 'The stone the builders rejected has become the cornerstone' (Luke 20:17). Her prayer foresees that the Anointed One will, in the words of the King James and English Standard versions of the Bible, 'turn the world upside down' (see Acts 17:6).

Pause to ponder
- What principles modelled by Hannah and Mary's prayers could you incorporate more fully into your prayer life?
- Which aspects of your life do you look forward to being reversed, and which would you prefer to stay unchanged?

Day 9
O holy night!

The LORD declares to you that the LORD himself will establish a house for you: when your days are over and you rest with your ancestors, I will raise up your offspring to succeed you, your own flesh and blood, and I will establish his kingdom. He is the one who will build a house for my Name, and I will establish the throne of his kingdom for ever. I will be his father, and he shall be my son. When he does wrong, I will punish him with a rod wielded by men, with floggings inflicted by human hands. But my love will never be taken away from him, as I took it away from Saul, whom I removed from before you. Your house and your kingdom will endure for ever before me; your throne shall be established for ever. (2 Samuel 7:11–16)

Quick glance

King David was disturbed and shared his concerns with Nathan the prophet: 'Here I am, *dwelling* in a *house* of cedar, while the ark of God *dwells* in a tent.' That night, the word of the Lord came to Nathan: the Lord promised to establish David's kingdom and throne for ever. Significantly, the words 'to dwell', 'house', and 'tabernacle' or 'dwelling-place' are repeated throughout the chapter. The New Testament reveals that the king who is to reign for ever is the Word who 'became flesh and made his *dwelling* among us' – who *tabernacled* among us. Devastatingly, God also reveals to David: 'When he *is caused to be guilty of iniquity*, I will cause him to be judged with the rod of men, with the stripes of the sons of man.' Incredibly, to preserve our lives, God will make 'him who

Day 9

had no sin to be sin for us'. Yet 'if, by the trespass of the one man, death reigned through that one man, how much more will those who receive God's abundant provision of grace and of the gift of righteousness reign in life through the one man, Jesus Christ!'

In-depth reflection

Many Christmas cards depict night-time settings. As we shall see in the coming days, symbolically this is perfectly correct. For the prophets foretold that 'on those living in the land of deep darkness a light has dawned' (Isaiah 9:2). This theme is also picked up by the eyewitnesses of Jesus. John begins his account, for example, with the words: 'The light shines in the darkness, and the darkness has not overcome it' (John 1:5).

To some degree, the night-time scenes also accurately reflect the historical record. Luke records that news of the Messiah's birth in Bethlehem was first revealed to 'shepherds living out in the fields near by, keeping watch over their flocks at night' (Luke 2:8). We also know that the star that prompted the eastern magi to seek the newborn king of the Jews 'stopped over the place where the child was' (Matthew 2:9). Some have proposed that the 'star' was in fact a comet, recorded by the Chinese for over seventy days in 5 BC.[1] If this were indeed the case, then this would not necessarily require the magi to have arrived at the family's home by night – dawn might even be more likely – but neither is the possibility ruled out. The one scene that Matthew definitely records as taking place by night is Joseph's rushed escape to Egypt with 'the child and his mother'. This follows the appearance to him in a dream of an angel of the Lord, who warned Joseph: 'Herod is going to search for the child to kill him' (Matthew 2:13–14).

The first significant night-time setting for news about Jesus, however, came centuries earlier. Of course, the darkness–light theme began earlier still – right at the start of the Bible:

---

1 E.g. C. J. Humphreys, 'The Star of Bethlehem a Comet in 5-BC and the Date of the Birth of Christ', *Quarterly Journal of the Royal Astronomical Society*, vol. 32, no. 4 (1991), p. 389.

In the beginning God created the heavens and the earth. Now the earth was formless and empty, darkness was over the surface of the deep, and the Spirit of God was hovering over the waters.

And God said, 'Let there be light,' and there was light. (Genesis 1:1–3)

We also noticed (on day 8) how Hannah spoke of this darkness in the context of the Lord's judgement: 'the wicked will be silenced in the place of darkness' (1 Samuel 2:9). Yet, in connection with the birth of the Messiah, we must look to the reign of King David.

Initially, David seemed to be the fulfilment of God's promise to Abraham that he would make 'kings of peoples' (Genesis 17:16) come from him and Sarah (as we saw on day 2). The Lord had also sworn to Abraham that his descendants would 'take possession of the cities of their enemies' (Genesis 22:17). Later, at the end of his life, Jacob told Judah: 'your hand will be on the neck of your enemies' (Genesis 49:8). We also saw (on day 5), how Balaam foretold that a ruler would one day 'come out of Jacob' (Numbers 24:17). All these promises were seen to be satisfied in David: 'David knew that the LORD had established him as king over Israel and had exalted his kingdom for the sake of his people Israel' (2 Samuel 5:12). 'The king was settled in his palace and the LORD had given him rest from all his enemies around him' (2 Samuel 7:1).

At that time, God's presence among his people was symbolised by the ark of God, 'which is called by the Name, the name of the LORD Almighty' (2 Samuel 6:2). That symbol had recently been brought to the City of David. Yet King David was disturbed. So he shared his concerns with Nathan the prophet: 'Here I am, living in a house of cedar, while the ark of God remains in a tent.' Initially, Nathan reassured the king: 'Whatever you have in mind, go ahead and do it, for the LORD is with you' (2 Samuel 7:2–3). That night, however, the word of the Lord came to the prophet:

Go and tell my servant David … 'Are you the one to build me a house to dwell in? I have not dwelt in a house from the

Day 9

day I brought the Israelites up out of Egypt to this day. I have been moving from place to place with a tent as my dwelling. Wherever I have moved with all the Israelites, did I ever say to any of their rulers whom I commanded to shepherd my people Israel, "Why have you not built me a house of cedar?"'
(2 Samuel 7:5–7)

The significance of this night-time revelation from the Lord is heightened in the original Hebrew, as the words 'to dwell' and 'house' are repeated throughout the chapter – six and fifteen times, respectively. Thus, translated literally, verse 1 began: 'When the king was *dwelling* in his *house* …' In verse 2, the king told the prophet: 'Here I am, *dwelling* in a *house* of cedar, while the ark of God *dwells* in a tent.'

After Nathan reported all the words of the Lord to David, the king 'went in and [*dwelt*] before the LORD' (v. 18), saying:

> Who am I, Sovereign LORD, and what is my family, that you have brought me this far? And as if this were not enough in your sight, Sovereign LORD, you have also spoken about the future of the house of your servant – and this decree, Sovereign LORD, is *for the human race*!
> (2 Samuel 7:18–19, alternative translation)

Significantly, God's response to David also includes another related word – 'tabernacle' or 'dwelling-place' – used three times:

> I have been moving from place to place with a tent as my [*tabernacle*] … I will provide a place for my people Israel and will plant them so that they can have a [*tabernacle*] of their own and no longer be disturbed … When your days are over and you [*tabernacle*] with your ancestors, I will raise up your offspring to succeed you, your own flesh and blood, and I will establish his kingdom.
> (2 Samuel 7:6, 10, 12)

O holy night!

So the promised King of Judah offers to build the Creator God a dwelling-place on earth. In response, the Lord promises to establish David's kingdom and throne for ever. Note, in verses 13 and 16 (see below), the connection with the '*throne* of honour' to be inherited by the needy in Hannah's prayer (explored on day 8), who are to be seated with princes.

Initially, God's promises clearly concern David's immediate successor, his son Solomon. It is David's own offspring who will succeed him. It is the king's 'own flesh and blood', the Lord says, 'who will build a house for my Name'. After this, however, the time frame of God's promise extends well beyond the life span of any single human:

> I will establish the throne of his kingdom for ever … my love will never be taken away from him … Your house and your kingdom shall endure for ever before me; your throne shall be established for ever.
> (2 Samuel 7:13, 15, 16)

This must refer once more to the Anointed King about whom Hannah spoke in her prayer – that is, the Messiah. In the New Testament, we see that this Messiah is the child who came down from heaven to give life to the world. He is the Word who 'became flesh and made his *dwelling* among us' (John 1:14) – that is, who *tabernacled* among us. At the very end of time, when this first heaven and first earth have passed away, we are told that 'God's *dwelling-place* is now among the people, and he will *dwell* with them. They will be his people, and God himself will be with them and be their God' (Revelation 21:3).

Yet, before then, we must notice a less triumphant note. Symbolically, it is fitting that it is revealed at night. For the Lord chose to speak again when darkness reigned. In the midst of his glorious promise to David of an everlasting kingdom, God reveals something else. As Hannah intimated, it is not by strength that the Anointed One will prevail, for the Lord says: 'I will be his father, and he shall be my son. When he does wrong, I will punish him

Day 9

with a rod wielded by men, with floggings inflicted by human hands' (2 Samuel 7:14).

The first sentence in the above verse is a powerful glimpse into the relationship between the God of Israel and the Messiah. The one who would come down from heaven to Bethlehem would be God's Son. The second sentence, in the original Hebrew, is even more remarkable. For it could be rendered in English as: 'When he *is caused to be guilty of iniquity*, I will cause him to be judged with the rod of men, with the stripes of the sons of man.'[2]

In the beginning (day 1) we saw that 'sin came into the world through one man, and death through sin, and so death spread to all [human beings]' (Romans 5:12 ESV). The Law of Moses has prepared us to expect the miraculous birth of a future deliverer so that we might somehow live through him. The one separated for this task, from the womb to the day of his death, we have been told is none other than the Anointed King who will judge the nations in righteousness.

With devastating detail, God now begins to reveal the means by which our lives might be preserved. Incredibly, God will make 'him who had no sin to be sin for us' (2 Corinthians 5:21). As the prophet Isaiah tells us:

> He was pierced for our transgressions,
>   he was crushed for our iniquities;
> the punishment that brought us peace was on him,
>   and by his wounds we are healed.
> We all, like sheep, have gone astray,
>   each of us has turned to our own way;
> and the LORD has laid on him
>   the iniquity of us all.
> (Isaiah 53:5–6)

Yet 'if, by the trespass of the one man, death reigned through that one man, how much more will those who receive God's abundant

---

[2] See Bernard Northrup, *Recognizing Messiah in the Psalms* (Fairfax, VA: Xulon Press, 2003), p.315.

provision of grace and of the gift of righteousness reign in life through the one man, Jesus Christ!' (Romans 5:17). Like Hannah and Mary, it is enough to make one want to burst out in praise! Words from the Christmas carol 'What Child Is This?' capture something of the wonder, 'magic' and immensity of it all:

> Nails, spear shall pierce Him through,
> The cross be borne for me, for you.
> Hail, hail the Word made flesh,
> The Babe, the Son of Mary.[3]

Pause to ponder
- What difference do you think it should make knowing that God's people 'are being built together to become a dwelling in which God lives by his Spirit' (Ephesians 2:22)?
- How might these truths help you to live more fully in the grace and righteousness of Christ?

---

[3] From 'What Child Is This?' (1865) by William Chatterton Dix, Hymnary.org: https://hymnary.org/text/what_child_is_this_who_laid_to_rest (accessed 29 January 2022).

Day 10
A testimony of warning

Nevertheless, there will be no more gloom for those who were in distress. In the past he humbled the land of Zebulun and the land of Naphtali, but in the future he will honour Galilee of the nations, by the Way of the Sea, beyond the Jordan –

The people walking in darkness
   have seen a great light;
on those living in the land of deep darkness
   a light has dawned.
You have enlarged the nation
   and increased their joy;
they rejoice before you
   as people rejoice at the harvest,
as warriors rejoice
   when dividing the plunder.
For as in the day of Midian's defeat,
   you have shattered
the yoke that burdens them,
   the bar across their shoulders,
   the rod of their oppressor.
Every warrior's boot used in battle
   and every garment rolled in blood
will be destined for burning,
   will be fuel for the fire.
For to us a child is born,
   to us a son is given,
   and the government will be on his shoulders.
And he will be called

A testimony of warning

> Wonderful Counsellor, Mighty God,
>   Everlasting Father, Prince of Peace.
> Of the greatness of his government and peace
>   there will be no end.
> He will reign on David's throne
>   and over his kingdom,
> establishing and upholding it
>   with justice and righteousness
>   from that time on and for ever.
> The zeal of the LORD Almighty
>   will accomplish this.
>
> (Isaiah 9:1–7)

Quick glance

Isaiah talks of a people walking in darkness and living in deep darkness – a word used elsewhere as a euphemism for death. For whom is the prophet's promise intended, though? When Matthew quotes this passage at the start of Jesus' ministry as a preacher, he sounds deliberately anachronistic – even insensitive or politically incorrect. Isaiah clarifies that those who do not consult this 'testimony of warning' and God's instruction will 'see only distress and darkness and fearful gloom, and they will be thrust into utter darkness'. 'Nevertheless', Isaiah continues, in the very place where the exile of God's chosen people began, he will cause a new light to dawn over the peoples of *all* nations. The promise of Isaiah 9 is for all those living under the curse, not just the Israelites. We, who otherwise face the utter darkness of death, can have certainty about this, 'for to us a child is born, to us a son is given'. More than this, the birth of this Prophet like Moses will bring us joy, freedom and peace.

In-depth reflection

Isaiah 9 is one of those passages with which many of us are overly familiar. We think we know what it is about because every year we

Day 10

hear it read and even sung. In many ways, it brings together many of the themes that we have seen building up in this Advent adventure as we have worked through the earlier passages.

Isaiah talks of a people walking in darkness and living in deep darkness. The first word for 'darkness' in the original Hebrew is the one used to describe what preceded God's creation of the universe. It depicts a state without life, without matter or even energy:

> In the beginning God created the heavens and the earth. Now the earth was formless and empty, darkness was over the surface of the deep, and the Spirit of God was hovering over the waters.
>
> And God said, 'Let there be light,' and there was light. God saw that the light was good, and he separated the light from the darkness. God called the light 'day,' and the darkness he called 'night.'
> (Genesis 1:1–5)

Isaiah's word for 'deep darkness' is elsewhere used as a euphemism for death. It occurs most frequently in the book of Job. For example, 'Have the *gates of death* been revealed to you, or have you seen the *gates of **deep darkness**?*' (Job 38:17 ESV). It also appears in the Psalms, where it is translated as the 'shadow of death', most famously in Psalm 23:4. This is where our tale of Christmas began – with the problem of death.

Isaiah goes on to foretell the birth of a child who will establish the kingdom of David for ever. We have noted already (on day 7) the connection between this passage and the account of events preceding the birth of Samson, how the name of the angel of the Lord was 'beyond understanding'. Here we are reminded that the promised Prophet like Moses will be a miraculously born deliverer anointed to reign on David's throne.

Yet we should slow down a second. Who is it that Isaiah says were in distress? For whom is the prophet's promise intended? When Matthew quotes this passage at the start of Jesus' ministry as a preacher, he highlights the geographic and historic context:

A testimony of warning

> When Jesus heard that John had been put in prison, he withdrew to Galilee. Leaving Nazareth, he went and lived in Capernaum, which was by the lake in the area of Zebulun and Naphtali – to fulfil what was said through the prophet Isaiah …
> (Matthew 4:12–14)

When Isaiah refers to the lands of Zebulun and Naphtali being humbled, he is referring to the exile, as they were the first tribes of Israel to be deported from the land formerly promised to Abraham. These events happened during the years when Isaiah was a prophet. We saw (on day 2) that he foretold the birth to a young woman of a boy who would be called Immanuel. 'Before the boy knows enough to reject the wrong and choose the right', the lands of Aram and Israel would be laid waste (Isaiah 7:14–17). In the following chapter, Isaiah records the birth of the auspicious son:

> I made love to the prophetess, and she conceived and gave birth to a son. And the Lord said to me, 'Name him Maher-Shalal-Hash-Baz. For before the boy knows how to say "My father" or "My mother", the wealth of Damascus and the plunder of Samaria will be carried off by the king of Assyria.'
> (Isaiah 8:3–4)

What follows is a warning that the Lord was about to bring the king of Assyria against those who rejoiced over the kings of Aram and Israel – namely, Rezin and Pekah son of Remaliah. We learn elsewhere that it was during Pekah's reign that Tiglath-Pileser III, king of Assyria, came and 'took Gilead and Galilee, including all the land of Naphtali, and deported the people to Assyria' (2 Kings 15:29). Later, after deporting the rest of the northern tribes of Israel, 'the king of Assyria brought people from Babylon, Kuthah, Avva, Hamath and Sepharvaim and settled them in the towns of Samaria to replace the Israelites' (2 Kings 17:24). We may be unfamiliar with the names of all these peoples. The point is clear, though. From that time on, the area ceased to be part of Israel and was instead populated by predominantly pagan peoples.

So, writing some seven centuries later, Matthew sounds deliberately anachronistic. In some ways, he is even being insensitive or politically incorrect. It is as though someone today declared, 'He withdrew to the mid-Atlantic states. Leaving Washington, DC, he went and lived in Philadelphia, in the area of the Iroquois and Shawnee.' There is a move in the USA to refer to regions in a way that acknowledges the enduring relationship that exists between Native Americans and their territories. Nevertheless, we would no more refer to states such as New York and Pennsylvania solely by the names of the Native nations and peoples of the region than Matthew's contemporaries would refer to 'the area of Zebulun and Naphtali'. To find out why Matthew highlights the time and place when God sent his people into exile, we need to return to Isaiah, where the prophet is warned not to follow the way of the people of Israel:

Do not call conspiracy
    everything this people calls a conspiracy;
do not fear what they fear,
    and do not dread it.
The LORD Almighty is the one you are to regard as holy,
    he is the one you are to fear,
    he is the one you are to dread.
He will be a holy place;
    for both Israel and Judah he will be
a stone that causes people to stumble
    and a rock that makes them fall.
And for the people of Jerusalem
    he will be a trap and a snare.
Many of them will stumble;
    they will fall and be broken,
    they will be snared and captured.
(Isaiah 8:12–15)

A testimony of warning

Hannah had us anticipate (on day 8) the King of whom it is written, 'The stone the builders rejected has become the cornerstone' (Luke 20:17). Here, Isaiah is more explicit. Later, he clarifies that the Lord will 'lay a stone in Zion, a tested stone, a precious cornerstone for a sure foundation; the one who relies on it will never be stricken with panic' (Isaiah 28:16). Those who do not consult this 'testimony of warning' and God's instruction 'will curse their king and their God' (Isaiah 8:16, 20–1). They will 'see only distress and darkness and fearful gloom, and they will be thrust into utter darkness' (Isaiah 8:22).

'Nevertheless,' Isaiah continues. '*Nevertheless*, there will be no more gloom for those who were in distress' (Isaiah 9:1). Isaiah now reveals that God, who said, 'Let light shine out of darkness' (2 Corinthians 4:6), will establish for ever his kingdom of justice and righteousness – or rightness with God. In the very place where the exile of God's chosen people began, he will cause a new light to dawn over the peoples of *all* the nations. Matthew's emphasis on the lands of Zebulun and Naphtali stresses that the promise of Isaiah 9 is for all those living under the curse, not just the Israelites. We, who otherwise face the utter darkness of death, can have certainty about this, 'for to us a child is born, to us a son is given'.

More than this, the birth of this Prophet like Moses will bring us joy, freedom and peace. This Prince of Peace will increase our joy and shatter the yoke that burdens us, and of his peace there will be no end! Incredibly, none of this depends on anything that we are able to do. The just and righteous zeal of the Lord Almighty alone will accomplish this.

Pause to ponder

- How uncomfortable or reassuring do you find Isaiah's warning that those who do not 'consult God's instruction and the testimony of warning' will 'see only distress and darkness and fearful gloom', but that for those who do, 'there will be no more gloom'?
- In what ways are you tempted to achieve your own joy, freedom and peace rather than patiently relying on God more fully?

Day 11
The coming Redeemer

Arise, shine, for your light has come,
    and the glory of the Lord rises upon you.
See, darkness covers the earth
    and thick darkness is over the peoples,
but the Lord rises upon you
    and his glory appears over you.
Nations will come to your light,
    and kings to the brightness of your dawn.

Lift up your eyes and look about you:
    all assemble and come to you;
your sons come from afar,
    and your daughters are carried on the hip.
Then you will look and be radiant,
    your heart will throb and swell with joy;
the wealth on the seas will be brought to you,
    to you the riches of the nations will come.
Herds of camels will cover your land,
    young camels of Midian and Ephah.
And all from Sheba will come,
    bearing gold and incense
    and proclaiming the praise of the Lord.
All Kedar's flocks will be gathered to you,
    the rams of Nebaioth will serve you;
they will be accepted as offerings on my altar,
    and I will adorn my glorious temple.
(Isaiah 60:1–7)

Quick glance

Isaiah 60 explicitly addresses a singular 'you'. This begs the question: who does the passage have in mind? In chapter 58, the prophet complains how 'no one calls for justice ... The way of peace they do not know.' To their credit, the people confess that they have turned their backs on God, incited oppression and uttered lies. Incredibly, Isaiah tells us that God achieves salvation for his people by repaying 'wrath to his enemies'. God himself will purchase our freedom. From the east to the west, all 'who repent of their sins' will revere the name of the Lord. The promised Redeemer of Isaiah 59:20, then, is the one to whom the following verses, in Isaiah 60, are primarily addressed. Nations will come to his light. So the camels depicted in our nativity scenes should remind us that God himself has achieved justice and deliverance for us. Those who 'repent of their sins' will serve in the new city of God, where the Lord himself will be our 'everlasting light' and our 'days of sorrow will end'.

In-depth reflection

Every Christmas our family receives at least one Christmas card that portrays the magi travelling on camels. As with the portrayal of nativity donkeys (which we considered on day 5), the Gospel writers tell us nothing about the means by which the visiting religious scholars might have travelled from the east. In fact, the closest we get to a camel in the four accounts of Jesus' life is the clothing worn by the Baptiser John.

Nevertheless, there are some tentative grounds for supposing that the eastern magi adopted this means of transport. We must look to the Old Testament, however, to find it – here in Isaiah 60: 'Herds of camels will cover your land, young camels of Midian and Ephah.' Without looking at the context, though, it is not immediately obvious that this necessarily has anything to do with Jesus' nativity.

The chapter explicitly addresses a singular 'you'. As the old King James Version made clear: 'Arise, shine; for *thy* light is come, and

Day 11

the glory of the LORD is risen upon *thee*.' This begs the question: who does the passage have in mind? To find the answer, we must look at the previous couple of chapters.

In chapter 58, the Lord instructs Isaiah to 'declare to my people their rebellion and to the descendants of Jacob their sins.' The prophet then asserts that 'the arm of the LORD is not too short to save, nor his ear too dull to hear'. Yet, addressing God's people in the plural, he goes on to lament: 'your iniquities have separated you from your God; your sins have hidden his face from you, so that he will not hear' (Isaiah 59:1–2).

In verses 4–8 he then complains how 'no one calls for justice … The way of peace they do not know; there is no justice in their paths.' To their credit, the people respond by acknowledging their fault:

So justice is far from us,
    and righteousness does not reach us.
We look for light, but all is darkness;
    for brightness, but we walk in deep shadows.
Like the blind we grope along the wall,
    feeling our way like people without eyes.
At midday we stumble as if it were twilight;
    among the strong, we are like the dead.
We all growl like bears;
    we moan mournfully like doves.
We look for justice, but find none;
    for deliverance, but it is far away.

For our offences are many in your sight,
    and our sins testify against us.
Our offences are ever with us,
    and we acknowledge our iniquities:
rebellion and treachery against the LORD,
    turning our backs on our God,
inciting revolt and oppression,
    uttering lies our hearts have conceived.

So justice is driven back,
    and righteousness stands at a distance;
truth has stumbled in the streets,
    honesty cannot enter.
Truth is nowhere to be found,
    and whoever shuns evil becomes a prey.
(Isaiah 59:9–15)

As before, we see the language of darkness and 'deep shadows' twinned with death. In chapter 9, Isaiah foretold (as we saw on day 10) that 'on those living in the land of deep darkness a light has dawned'. Yet here the people 'look for light, but all is darkness'. In chapter 9 he foresaw that the kingdom of David would be established and upheld with justice and righteousness for ever. Yet here the people confess that they have turned their backs on God, incited oppression and uttered lies. They recognise that 'justice is driven back, and righteousness stands at a distance'.

Isaiah goes on to reveal that the Lord also 'looked and was displeased that there was no justice. He saw that there was no one, he was appalled that there was no one to intervene' (Isaiah 59:15–16). Dramatically, however, we then see God himself intervene:

So his own arm achieved salvation for him,
    and his own righteousness sustained him.
He put on righteousness as his breastplate,
    and the helmet of salvation on his head;
he put on the garments of vengeance
    and wrapped himself in zeal as in a cloak.
According to what they have done,
    so will he repay
wrath to his enemies
    and retribution to his foes;
    he will repay the islands their due.
From the west, people will fear the name of the LORD,
    and from the rising of the sun, they will revere his glory.
For he will come like a pent-up flood

Day 11

    that the breath of the Lord drives along.
'The Redeemer will come to Zion,
    to those in Jacob who repent of their sins,'
        declares the Lord.
(Isaiah 59:16–20)

As, again, we saw (yesterday), 'the zeal of the Lord Almighty will accomplish this' (Isaiah 9:7). Elsewhere, the word 'zeal' is typically translated 'jealousy'. It conveys extreme passion and is often associated with vengeance. For example, in Proverbs we read: 'For *jealousy* arouses a husband's fury, and he will show no mercy when he takes revenge' (Proverbs 6:34). Here in Isaiah 59, the Lord's zeal is associated with righteousness and salvation, as well as with vengeance.

We find a graphic illustration of this zeal in the days of Moses, when Israel was being led astray by the people of Moab. The men of Israel 'began to indulge in sexual immorality with Moabite women, who invited them to the sacrifices to their gods. The people ate the sacrificial meal and bowed down before these gods' (Numbers 25:1–2). This caused the Lord's anger to burn against them. Yet, even as the leaders were discussing how to deal with the problem, some continued in their rebellion:

> Then an Israelite man brought into the camp a Midianite woman right before the eyes of Moses and the whole assembly of Israel while they were weeping at the entrance to the tent of meeting. When Phinehas son of Eleazar, the son of Aaron, the priest, saw this, he left the assembly, took a spear in his hand and followed the Israelite into the tent. He drove the spear into both of them, right through the Israelite man and into the woman's stomach. Then the plague against the Israelites was stopped; but those who died in the plague numbered 24,000.
> (Numbers 25:6–9)

By means of this act, the Lord tells Moses, Phinehas 'turned my anger away from the Israelites. Since he was as *zealous* for my honour among them as I am, I did not put an end to them in my *zeal*' (Numbers 25:11). Instead of vengeance, God makes a covenant of peace with Phinehas: 'He and his descendants will have a covenant of a lasting priesthood, because he was *zealous* for the honour of his God and made atonement for the Israelites' (Numbers 25:13).

Incredibly, Isaiah tells us, by repaying 'wrath to his enemies' God achieves salvation for his people. To those 'who repent of their sins', the Redeemer will come. No other human can help us. No Phinehas can intervene on our behalf. We are all 'like the blind' leading the blind. 'Our offences are ever with us.' Yet, Isaiah reveals, God himself will purchase our freedom. As he told the Israelites when they were slaves to the Egyptians: 'I will *free* you from being slaves to them, and I will *redeem* you with an outstretched arm and with mighty acts of judgment' (Exodus 6:6). He will come to 'Zion', but his redemption is not just for 'Jacob'. From the east to the west – that is, from across the whole world – all who repent of their sins will revere the name of the Lord. For, just as the Lord 'blew with [his] breath' and 'brought the waters of the sea back over [Pharaoh and his army]' (Exodus 15:10, 19), so too will the Redeemer 'come like a pent-up flood that the breath of the LORD drives along' (Isaiah 59:19)!

The promised Redeemer of Isaiah 59:20, then, is the one to whom the following verses, in Isaiah 60, are primarily addressed. The prophet's continuing vision concerns the time when this Redeemer's light has come, when the glory of the Lord appears over him. Nations will come to his light. The riches of the nations will be brought to him. 'Herds of camels will cover your land, young camels of Midian and Ephah. And all from Sheba will come, bearing gold and incense and proclaiming the praise of the LORD' (Isaiah 60:6).

As symbolic representatives of the nations, the magi travelled from the east. 'They saw the child with his mother Mary, and they bowed down and worshipped him. Then they opened their treasures and presented him with gifts of gold, frankincense and myrrh' (Matthew 2:11). So the camels depicted in our nativity

Day 11

scenes should remind us that God himself has achieved justice and deliverance for us. Our Redeemer has come. We simply need to acknowledge the ways in which we have turned our backs on God. Those of us who 'repent of [our] sins' can be confident that his Spirit will not depart from us and his words will always be on our lips 'from this time on and for ever' (Isaiah 59:21).

'The nation or kingdom that will not serve [the Lord] will perish; it will be utterly ruined' (Isaiah 60:12). The alternative is to serve in the new city of God, with its walls of salvation and gates of praise (Isaiah 60:18). Built around our Saviour and Redeemer, 'the Mighty One of Jacob', we can look ahead to the new Jerusalem, as spoken of in the book of Revelation, where the Lord himself will be our 'everlasting light' and our 'days of sorrow will end' (Isaiah 60:16, 20).

Pause to ponder

- Thinking of specific examples of injustice experienced in both your own life and the world at large, how does God's coming to uphold justice give you hope?
- In what specific ways could the verses we have reflected on today guide how you pray concerning the injustices you have identified – those both large and small?

Day 12
Twisted lyrics

Cursed is the one who trusts in man,
   who draws strength from mere flesh
   and whose heart turns away from the Lord.
That person will be like a bush in the wastelands;
   they will not see prosperity when it comes.
They will dwell in the parched places of the desert,
   in a salt land where no one lives.

But blessed is the one who trusts in the Lord,
   whose confidence is in him.
They will be like a tree planted by the water
   that sends out its roots by the stream.
It does not fear when heat comes;
   its leaves are always green.
It has no worries in a year of drought
   and never fails to bear fruit.
(Jeremiah 17:5–8)

Quick glance

Jeremiah 17 begins with a reminder that God's people have turned away from him and his promised blessings. We need the Prophet like Moses – the promised Messiah – to free us. For our iniquities have separated us from God and we are enslaved by our own folly. The prophet Jeremiah presents us with the same choice as did Isaiah. We can either trust in human beings or we can trust in the Lord. If we trust in ourselves, those around us or even our leaders, then we will ultimately be 'like a bush in the wastelands'.

Alternatively, if we trust in the Lord, then we will be those whose 'leaves are always green'. We will never fail to bear fruit. Yet, in our enthusiasm to welcome the Christ-child, we should also recall that the Redeemer will 'come like a pent-up flood that the breath of the LORD drives along'. The apostle Paul and the early church also recognised that God's provision of eternal life and salvation necessarily means judgement and destruction for others: 'If anyone does not love the Lord, let that person be cursed! Come, Lord!'

In-depth reflection

Several years ago, I taught English as a foreign language to adults in Central Asia. A colleague who had previously taught in India recounted how a group of students once asked her about a Christmas song they had heard. 'What does it mean', they asked, 'that "The leaves never die"?' At first, she had no idea what they were talking about. Only when they sang the Christmas classic did she realise that they had misheard the words. The words were in fact Spanish and the song was José Feliciano's 'Feliz Navidad'!

There are, of course, other Christmas songs that genuinely do feature trees. On this twelfth day of Advent, we could mention 'The Twelve Days of Christmas' with its 'partridge in a pear tree'. Except that those twelve days refer to the ones that follow Christmas, not these that precede it.

Then there's 'Jesus Christ the Apple Tree', which originated as a poem, 'The Tree of Life My Soul Hath Seen'. This is said to be an allusion to Song of Songs 2:3: 'Like an apple tree among the trees of the forest is my beloved among the young men.' The carol was probably an attempt to transform the Twelfth Night tradition of wassailing. This was a pagan custom in which Ancient Britons visited orchards and sang to the spirits of the trees. This, they hoped, would secure a good harvest in the year ahead.

Neither of these, however, has anything to do with the fruitless fir trees that many of us bring into our homes at the end of every year. Reportedly, this custom began centuries ago in northern Europe, and the early trees were decorated with apples and other edible treats. According to the *Encyclopaedia Britannica*:

> Evergreen trees became part of Christian rites in Germany, and in the Middle Ages 'paradise trees' began to appear there. Meant to represent the Garden of Eden, these evergreen trees were hung with apples and displayed in homes on December 24, the religious feast day of Adam and Eve. Other decorations were added – Martin Luther reportedly first hung lighted candles on a tree in the 16th century – and paradise trees evolved into Christmas trees.[1]

Either way, it is perhaps noteworthy that there is no paradise tree, Christmas tree or any other fir tree in *A Christmas Carol* by Charles Dickens, published in 1843. That is to say, it is a more modern tradition that resembles some earlier customs but finds its origins and significance elsewhere.

All that being said, the Bible *does* picture a tree whose leaves never die. By a curious coincidence, the passage even goes on to mention a partridge: 'Like a partridge that hatches eggs it did not lay are those who gain riches by unjust means. When their lives are half gone, their riches will desert them, and in the end they will prove to be fools' (Jeremiah 17:11).

The chapter begins with a reminder that God's people have turned away from him and his promised blessings:

> Judah's sin is engraved with an iron tool,
>   inscribed with a flint point,
> on the tablets of their hearts
>   and on the horns of their altars.
> Even their children remember
>   their altars and Asherah poles

---

[1] Amy Tikkanen, 'How Did the Tradition of Christmas Trees Start?', Britannica (no date): https://www.britannica.com/story/how-did-the-tradition-of-christmas-trees-start (accessed 7 February 2022).

Day 12

> beside the spreading trees
>   and on the high hills.
> My mountain in the land
>   and your wealth and all your treasures
> I will give away as plunder,
>   together with your high places,
>   because of sin throughout your country.
> Through your own fault you will lose
>   the inheritance I gave you.
> I will enslave you to your enemies
>   in a land you do not know,
> for you have kindled my anger,
>   and it will burn for ever.
> (Jeremiah 17:1–4)

We need the Prophet like Moses – the promised Messiah – to free us. For our iniquities have separated us from God and we are enslaved by our own folly. Our offences are many in his sight, and our sins testify against us. They are so much a part of our nature, it is as though our rebellion is tattooed with an iron tool on the tablets of our hearts.

The prophet Jeremiah then presents us with the same choice as did Isaiah. We can either trust in human beings or we can trust in the Lord. If we trust in ourselves, those around us or even our leaders, then we will ultimately be 'like a bush in the wastelands'. We will miss out on God's promised blessings and we 'will not see prosperity when it comes':

> All who forsake you will be put to shame.
> Those who turn away from you will be written in the dust
>   because they have forsaken the LORD,
>   the spring of living water.
> (Jeremiah 17:13)

Alternatively, if we trust in the Lord, then we will be 'like a tree planted by the water'. We will not fear when trials come. For we will be those whose 'leaves are always green'. We will never fail to bear fruit.

Yet 'the heart is deceitful above all things and beyond cure' (Jeremiah 17:9). As Moses and the earlier prophets have already made clear, the Lord is 'the hope of Israel' (v. 13). Only he can heal our scarred and deceitful hearts. Only he can save us. The only requirement demanded of us is that we place our confidence in him, that we live in daily expectation of his promised Redeemer: 'They keep saying to me, "Where is the word of the Lord? Let it now be fulfilled!"' (Jeremiah 15:15).

It is right that those of us who know the Lord look with eagerness for his return. Echoing the prayer of Manoah (which we saw on day 7) 'to let the man of God you sent to us come again' (Judges 13:8), we pray using the closing words of the Bible: 'Come, Lord Jesus' (Revelation 22:20). Yet, in our enthusiasm to welcome the Christ-child, we should also recall that the Redeemer will 'come like a pent-up flood that the breath of the Lord drives along' (Isaiah 59:19).

We are often those who, in the words of Isaiah, 'look for justice' (Isaiah 59:11). We see acts of injustice in the world around us and we long for justice. Or we feel that others have treated us unfairly and we want the wrong to be made right. 'Righteousness does not reach us' (Isaiah 59:9). Yet, although we long for God to restore order to our lives, we tend to shy away from what that means for the prevailing disorder. Not so Jeremiah. He prays unashamedly:

> Do not be a terror to me;
>   you are my refuge in the day of disaster.
> Let my persecutors be put to shame,
>   but keep me from shame;
> let them be terrified,
>   but keep me from terror.
> Bring on them the day of disaster;
>   destroy them with double destruction.
> (Jeremiah 17:17–18)

Day 12

His words echo some of the psalms of David. For instance, David prays:

> For your name's sake, LORD, preserve my life;
>   in your righteousness, bring me out of trouble.
> In your unfailing love, silence my enemies;
>   destroy all my foes,
>   for I am your servant.
> (Psalm 143:11–12)

The first psalm also describes 'the one who does not walk in step with the wicked' and 'whose delight is in the law of the LORD' as being 'like a tree planted by streams of water, which yields its fruit in season and whose leaf does not wither'. Such individuals are contrasted with 'the wicked', who 'are like chaff that the wind blows away', who 'will not stand in the judgment' and whose way 'leads to destruction' (Psalm 1:1–6).

The apostle Paul and the early Christians also recognised that God's provision of eternal life and salvation necessarily means judgement and destruction for others: 'If anyone does not love the Lord, let that person be cursed! Come, Lord!' (1 Corinthians 16:22). Like them, this insight should impel us to direct to the Lord those who have not yet been relieved of their fears and worries. For we whose 'leaves are always green' are now the means by which others can encounter the Giver of life. As the very end of the Bible portrays, using Jeremiah's image: 'On each side of the river stood the tree of life, bearing twelve crops of fruit, yielding its fruit every month. And the leaves of the tree are for the healing of the nations' (Revelation 22:2).

So, as we sweep up a few more fallen pine needles from under the Christmas tree, may our lives never fail to bear fruit for the Lord. If the Redeemer had not come, then we would remain on the wrong side of justice. We would 'not see prosperity when it comes'. As Christmas Day approaches, may our hearts turn afresh towards the coming Lord. Or, in the words of José Feliciano's misheard song, 'I wanna wish you a merry Christmas from the bottom of my heart.'

Pause to ponder
- In what ways might you be uncomfortable about the need for individuals to be judged if justice is to be fully achieved in the specific situations that you reflected on yesterday?
- In what ways and what areas of your life would you like to be more fruitful and more full of meaning – and what could you, by God's enabling, perhaps change to make this more likely?

Day 13
A new hope

This is what the LORD says:

> 'A voice is heard in Ramah,
>   mourning and great weeping,
> Rachel weeping for her children
>   and refusing to be comforted,
>   because they are no more.'

(Jeremiah 31:15)

Quick glance

There are plenty of verses in the Psalms and the Prophets about lamentation and the slaughter of innocents. Why did Matthew choose to quote this verse from Jeremiah instead of, say, Hosea 9:13: 'Ephraim will bring out their children to the slayer'? The context in Jeremiah makes clear that the prophet's focus is on restoration. God has seen his exiled people's plight and has heard their cries of despair. So he offers them words of comfort: 'There is hope!' *This* is the message of Jeremiah, of Matthew and of Christmas. Somehow, God will 'raise up' the king to whom he promised an everlasting kingdom and throne. Yet God reveals that his promised king will do more than just restore us. He will transform us. The Lord will make a new covenant with us. He will cause our minds and hearts no longer to be inclined to rebellion. Herod's slaughter of Bethlehem's infants is not a cause for despair. Instead, it is an invitation to be comforted. Jeremiah and Matthew would have us perceive that events such as those in Bethlehem serve as a guarantee: justice will ultimately be satisfied in full.

In-depth reflection

Where is Ramah? Why does Matthew quote this verse from Jeremiah after the magi's visit to Bethlehem? And how is it in any way relevant to the events surrounding the birth of Jesus?

It is tempting to dismiss Matthew's citation from Jeremiah in his nativity narrative as clumsy and unnecessary. It looks as though he has shoehorned a random proof-text for a bizarre and gruesome episode that appears to add little to our understanding of Christmas. The magi, having been sent by Herod to Bethlehem, have worshipped and presented their treasured gifts to the child born to be king of the Jews. Then, 'having been warned in a dream not to go back to Herod, they returned to their country by another route' (Matthew 2:12).

Matthew then recounts two dreams that prompt Joseph to 'take the child and his mother' first to Egypt and, at an unspecified time later, back to Israel. Both of these snippets make pointed reference to the death of Herod, which scholars date to 4 BC. Sandwiched between the two, Matthew records a murderous scene of the kind for which Herod is infamous:

> When Herod realised that he had been outwitted by the Magi, he was furious, and he gave orders to kill all the boys in Bethlehem and its vicinity who were two years old and under, in accordance with the time he had learned from the Magi. Then what was said through the prophet Jeremiah was fulfilled:
>
> 'A voice is heard in Ramah,
>   weeping and great mourning,
> Rachel weeping for her children
>   and refusing to be comforted,
>   because they are no more.'
>
> (Matthew 2:16–18)

Having established this overall context, the relevance of the Jeremiah citation is no clearer. There are plenty of verses in the Psalms and the Prophets about lamentation and the slaughter of innocents.

Day 13

Why would Matthew not choose, say, Hosea 9:13: 'Ephraim will bring out their children to the slayer'? This would seem to be more directly fulfilled by this episode. The context of that verse even conforms to the picture of judgement that we have seen associated with the promised Redeemer in the other prophets: 'The days of punishment are coming, the days of reckoning are at hand … because your sins are so many and your hostility so great' (Hosea 9:7).

So, what is so special about these words of Jeremiah that Matthew felt specifically compelled to incorporate them? Let's begin with Ramah. For, significantly, this was the home of Elkanah and Hannah and their son, Samuel the prophet (1 Samuel 1:19; 2:11; 7:17; 25:1). It is near 'Bethel in the hill country of Ephraim' (Judges 4:5). So the verse is associated geographically with one of the earlier miracle-born deliverers. It is also one of the places where the captives from Jerusalem and Judah were carried by the Babylonians when they were taken into exile (Jeremiah 40:1).

What of Rachel? She was the beloved wife of Jacob (also named Israel), the mother of Joseph and Benjamin. She died while travelling from Bethel 'and was buried on the way to Ephrath or Bethlehem' (Genesis 35:19). When Samuel anoints Israel's first king, he also tells us that Rachel's tomb is near 'Zelzah on the border of Benjamin' (1 Samuel 10:2). So, besides being one of the matriarchs of Israel, she also has ties to the area.

Why, though, did Jeremiah say she would not be comforted? In actual fact, the context of the passage makes clear that, unlike the verse from Hosea, this is *not* about judgement. Neither is it about persecution. Instead it is about restoration. The tribes of Israel had been taken into exile by the kings of Assyria and Babylon. So circumstances appeared hopeless. At this time, God promises to redeem his people:

'Hear the word of the Lord, you nations;
   proclaim it in distant coastlands:
"He who scattered Israel will gather them
   and will watch over his flock like a shepherd."
For the Lord will deliver Jacob

and redeem them from the hand of those stronger than they.
They will come and shout for joy on the heights of Zion;
> they will rejoice in the bounty of the LORD –
the grain, the new wine and the olive oil,
> the young of the flocks and herds.
They will be like a well-watered garden,
> and they will sorrow no more.
Then young women will dance and be glad,
> young men and old as well.
I will turn their mourning into gladness;
> I will give them comfort and joy instead of sorrow.
I will satisfy the priests with abundance,
> and my people will be filled with my bounty,'
>> declares the LORD.
(Jeremiah 31:10–14)

The prophet then interrupts this joyful message with the verse that Matthew highlights. In doing so, he shows that God has seen his people's plight and has heard their cries of despair – and heard them from the time that their distress began. He does not dwell for long, though, on their refusal to be comforted. Instead, he offers them words of comfort:

This is what the LORD says:

> 'Restrain your voice from weeping
>> and your eyes from tears,
> for your work will be rewarded,' declares the LORD.
>> 'They will return from the land of the enemy.
> So there is hope for your descendants,' declares the LORD.
>> 'Your children will return to their own land.'
(Jeremiah 31:16–17)

'There is hope!' *This* is the message of Jeremiah. *This* is the message of Matthew. And *this* is the marvellous and 'magical' message of Christmas. The relevant passage begins in chapter 30. Jeremiah is

Day 13

told to write in a book all the words that God has spoken to him. He begins by warning of a day of divine judgement:

> These are the words the LORD spoke concerning Israel and Judah: 'This is what the LORD says:
>
> "Cries of fear are heard –
>   terror, not peace …"'
>
> See, the storm of the LORD
>   will burst out in wrath,
> a driving wind swirling down
>   on the heads of the wicked.
> The fierce anger of the LORD will not turn back
>   until he fully accomplishes
>   the purposes of his heart.
> (Jeremiah 30:4–5, 23–4)

We ourselves have longed to see justice done in the world around us. How much more so must the righteous God desire the same? So justice must be executed. For, as Isaiah told us (on day 11), only then can God bring about our deliverance:

> How awful that day will be!
>   No other will be like it.
> It will be a time of trouble for Jacob,
>   but he will be saved out of it.
>
> 'In that day,' declares the LORD Almighty,
>   'I will break the yoke off their necks
> and will tear off their bonds;
>   no longer will foreigners enslave them.
> Instead, they will serve the LORD their God
>   and David their king,
>   whom I will raise up for them.'
> (Jeremiah 30:7–9)

A new hope

By the time of the exile, King David had been long dead. Yet Jeremiah reveals that, on the day when God saves and liberates his people, he will raise up David their king for them. Isaiah foresaw (as we read on day 10) that a miraculously born deliverer would reign on David's throne. Jeremiah seems to go further. Somehow, God will 'raise up' the king to whom he promised an everlasting kingdom and throne (see day 9).

Yet that is not all. If God were simply to restore us, then there is no reason why we would not, yet again, turn our backs on him. After all, that is the recurring plight of God's people, as recorded throughout the Old Testament. As God had earlier lamented through Jeremiah:

> From the time your ancestors left Egypt until now, day after day, again and again I sent you my servants the prophets. But they did not listen to me or pay attention. They were stiff-necked and did more evil than their ancestors.
> (Jeremiah 7:25–6)

So God reveals that his promised king will do more than just restore us. He will transform us:

> 'The days are coming,' declares the LORD,
>   'when I will make a new covenant
> with the people of Israel
>   and with the people of Judah.
> It will not be like the covenant
>   I made with their ancestors
> when I took them by the hand
>   to lead them out of Egypt,
> because they broke my covenant,
>   though I was a husband to them,'
>   declares the LORD.
> 'This is the covenant I will make with the people of Israel
>   after that time,' declares the LORD.
> 'I will put my law in their minds

Day 13

and write it on their hearts.
I will be their God,
   and they will be my people.
No longer will they teach their neighbour,
   or say to one another, "Know the Lord,"
because they will all know me,
   from the least of them to the greatest,'
      declares the Lord.
'For I will forgive their wickedness
   and will remember their sins no more.'
(Jeremiah 31:31–4)

This is the hope that Jeremiah proclaims to Rachel and that Matthew shares with us. The Lord will make a new covenant with us. He will cause our minds and hearts no longer to be inclined to rebellion. We will all know him – from the least of us to the greatest. When he raises up his promised Redeemer, he will forgive our wickedness and forget our sins. He will free us from all guilt and blame.

Herod's slaughter of Bethlehem's infants was, of course, a terrible loss for the dozen or so families who are believed to have been caught up in his fury. Yet, for the magi and all others who seek the Davidic king whom God promised to raise up, it is not a cause for despair. Instead, it is an invitation to be comforted.

We all too easily focus on the unjust world around us. Jeremiah and Matthew would have us perceive that events such as those in Bethlehem serve as a guarantee: justice will ultimately be satisfied in full. We can recognise in this episode that God's day of justice will be even more terrible for those who have turned their backs on him – those who have rebelled against his goodness. Yet we will be saved out of it. The Lord will be our God, and we will be his people. With Jeremiah and the magi, we 'sing with joy for Jacob' and 'shout for the foremost of the nations': 'Make your praises heard, and say, "Lord, save your people, the remnant of Israel"' (Jeremiah 31:7).

A new hope

Pause to ponder
- What comfort can you draw from Christ even in the examples of injustice that you reflected on over the last two days?
- In what ways do you think that the Lord has transformed your mind and heart throughout your life – and in what ways would you welcome further transformation?

Day 14
The messenger

You have wearied the LORD with your words.
'How have we wearied him?' you ask.
By saying, 'All who do evil are good in the eyes of the LORD, and he is pleased with them' or 'Where is the God of justice?'
'I will send my messenger, who will prepare the way before me. Then suddenly the Lord you are seeking will come to his temple; the messenger of the covenant, whom you desire, will come,' says the LORD Almighty.
But who can endure the day of his coming? Who can stand when he appears?
(Malachi 2:17 – 3:2)

Quick glance

In the final book of the Old Testament, we are told of another angel-messenger: the priests. They, however, show contempt for the Lord's name and complain, 'Where is the God of *justice?*' Confronted by their hypocrisy, God throws their own words back at them. The 'messenger of the covenant', whom they claim to desire (or '*delight in*'), will come – 'for judgment' or 'for *justice*'. This priestly messenger will prepare the people of God for his coming. If the Lord were 'suddenly to come to his temple' then we would all be consumed by his justice. The good news is not just about Jesus. It also significantly features his priestly messenger: John the Baptiser, son of the priest Zechariah. It is worth asking why God needed John to prepare the people for the Messiah's coming. The answer is surely similar to why he continues to use his people today: to prepare others to encounter him. The message of believers in every generation remains that of John, Christ, the twelve disciples and the early church: 'Repent and believe in Jesus!'

In-depth reflection

Is your Christmas tree topped by a star or an angel? Polls on both sides of the Atlantic indicate that about 2 in 5 of us put a star on top of our trees and about 1 in 4 an angel. Fewer than 1 in 10 choose something else, while the rest either don't have a tree, don't put anything at the top or don't know what they usually do.

On our journey to rediscover the 'magic' of Christmas, we have encountered only two stars. The first was that spoken of by Balaam (on day 5); the second was the heavenly body that led the magi (on day 9). On the other hand, angels appear aplenty. Think of those that spoke to Abraham and Sarah; or to Manoah and his wife (on day 2). Think also of those that appeared to Mary and Joseph, to the father of John the Baptiser and to the shepherds of Bethlehem.

The word 'angel' occurs 196 times in the Old Testament. Almost half the time, it is translated 'messenger' or 'envoy'. For instance, when Jacob returned to the promised land, after working for twenty years in Paddan Aram for Laban, 'the *angels* of God met him'; but, two verses later, we are told that he 'sent *messengers* ahead of him to his brother Esau' (Genesis 32:1, 3). Later, when Joshua destroyed the city of Jericho, the lives of Rahab the prostitute and her family were spared because she hid the *messengers* ('spies' in NIV) whom Israel had sent (Joshua 6:17, 25). It is also the word used when kings sent people to do certain tasks. For example, 'Saul sent *messengers* to Jesse and said, "Send me your son David, who is with the sheep"' (1 Samuel 16:19). Later, 'Hiram king of Tyre sent *envoys* to David, along with cedar logs and carpenters and stonemasons, and they built a palace for David' (2 Samuel 5:11).

In the final book of the Old Testament, we are told of another angel-messenger. In fact, the book itself is called 'My Angel' or

Day 14

'My Messenger' – Malachi in Hebrew. The identity of this particular messenger is given in chapter 2: 'the lips of a priest ought to preserve knowledge, because he is the *messenger* of the LORD Almighty and people seek instruction from his mouth' (Malachi 2:7). The priests being addressed, however, have been cursed because they 'violated the covenant with Levi' (Malachi 2:8). The Lord describes the latter warmly as 'a covenant of life and peace' (Malachi 2:5).

We noted this 'covenant of peace' in the context of the Lord's zeal (on day 11). Phinehas and his descendants, remember, were to have 'a covenant of a lasting priesthood' (Numbers 25:13) because he was zealous for the honour of God. In contrast, now the priests 'have not resolved to honour me' (Malachi 2:2). In fact, they even show contempt for the Lord's name (Malachi 1:6). So the Lord rebukes them and their descendants as a warning 'so that my covenant with Levi may continue' (Malachi 2:3–4). Nehemiah, probably writing around the same period, also mentioned those who 'defiled the priestly office and the covenant of the priesthood and of the Levites' (Nehemiah 13:29).

Yet the priests simply complain that the Lord 'no longer *looks with favour on* [their] offerings or *accepts* them with pleasure from [their] hands' (Malachi 2:13). Worse still, they claim that 'all who do evil are good in the eyes of the LORD' and that he *delights in* them (Malachi 2:17). If this sounds similar to some of the so-called 'truth' claims made in our own era, then so too does the next complaint: 'Where is the God of *justice*?' (Malachi 2:17).

It is right to long for justice. It is wrong, however, to think that God does not care. As we saw (on day 11), God is so appalled there is no justice that he promises to intervene. Confronted by the hypocrisy of the priests, he throws their own words (highlighted in the previous paragraph) back at them. The 'messenger of the covenant', whom they claim to 'desire' (or *delight in*), will come. The Lord Almighty will send his messenger, who will *turn towards* (*look with favour on*) or 'prepare the way before me. Then suddenly the Lord you are seeking will come to his temple' (Malachi 3:1). The God of justice, whom they claim to seek, will come. He will do so, however, he tells the priests, 'to put you on trial' (NIV) – 'for judgement' (ESV) or for *justice* (Malachi 3:5):

> He will purify the Levites and refine them like gold and silver. Then the LORD will have men who will bring offerings in righteousness, and the offerings of Judah and Jerusalem will be acceptable to the LORD, as in days gone by, as in former years.
> (Malachi 3:3–4)

So a priestly messenger is promised to prepare the people of God for his coming. If the Lord were 'suddenly' to come to his temple, we would all be consumed by his justice. 'Not a root or a branch' would be left to us (Malachi 4:1). The messenger is sent first, however, to call us to turn back to God. He gives us the opportunity to change our ways before it is too late: '"Ever since the time of your ancestors you have turned away from my decrees and have not kept them. Return to me, and I will return to you," says the LORD Almighty' (Malachi 3:7).

The final two verses of the book – indeed of the whole Old Testament – give us another insight into this promised priestly messenger:

> I will send the prophet Elijah to you before that great and dreadful day of the LORD comes. He will turn the hearts of the parents to their children, and the hearts of the children to their parents; or else I will come and strike the land with total destruction.
> (Malachi 4:5–6)

Importantly, the focus of this promise is not the messenger but the Lord for whom he prepares the way. Ultimately, we are God's children, and his messenger seeks to turn our hearts back to our heavenly Father.

As we turn the pages of the Bible to the New Testament, we find that this priestly messenger is explicitly identified as John the

Baptiser, son of the priest Zechariah. Jesus himself told the crowds that John was 'more than a prophet' (Matthew 11:9):

> This is the one about whom it is written:
>
> > 'I will send my messenger ahead of you,
> > who will prepare your way before you.'
>
> … And if you are willing to accept it, he is the Elijah who was to come.
> (Matthew 11:10, 14)

After Jesus went up a mountain with Peter, James and John and 'was transfigured before them' (Matthew 17:2), the disciples asked him why the teachers of the law taught that Elijah must come before the Son of Man:

> Jesus replied, 'To be sure, Elijah comes and will restore all things. But I tell you, Elijah has already come, and they did not recognise him, but have done to him everything they wished. In the same way the Son of Man is going to suffer at their hands.' Then the disciples understood that he was talking to them about John the Baptist.
> (Matthew 17:11–13)

Interestingly, a simple count reveals that 1 in 17 (5.9 per cent) of the verses in the four Gospel accounts refer to John and his ministry.[1] The good news is not just about Jesus but also significantly features his messenger. Mark's account even begins with John:

> The beginning of the good news about Jesus the Messiah, the Son of God, as it is written in Isaiah the prophet:

---

[1] To be exact: 58 out of 1,071 verses in Matthew; 33 out of 678 in Mark; 93 out of 1,151 in Luke; 39 out of 879 in John.

The messenger

> 'I will send my messenger ahead of you,
>   who will prepare your way' –
> 'a voice of one calling in the wilderness,
> "Prepare the way for the Lord,
>   make straight paths for him."'
>
> And so John the Baptist appeared in the wilderness, preaching a baptism of repentance for the forgiveness of sins.
> (Mark 1:1–4)

Luke informs us that John's father 'belonged to the priestly division of Abijah' and his mother Elizabeth 'was also a descendant of Aaron' (Luke 1:5). When Zechariah was on duty in the Temple, the angel that appeared to him used the words of Malachi to describe the work that John would do:

> He will bring back many of the people of Israel to the Lord their God. And he will go on before the Lord, in the spirit and power of Elijah, to turn the hearts of the parents to their children and the disobedient to the wisdom of the righteous – to make ready a people prepared for the Lord.
> (Luke 1:16–17)

The first two Gospel accounts suggest that Jesus began his public ministry in earnest after John had been arrested:

> After John was put in prison, Jesus went into Galilee, proclaiming the good news of God. 'The time has come,' he said. 'The kingdom of God has come near. Repent and believe the good news!'
> (Mark 1:14–15; compare Matthew 4:12)

This is strikingly similar to the message that John had been preaching: 'Repent, for the kingdom of heaven has come near' (Matthew 3:2). So it is unsurprising that, even at that time, there was some confusion distinguishing 'the messenger of the covenant'

Day 14

and 'the Lord'. For instance, when Jesus asked his disciples who people said he was, they replied: 'Some say John the Baptist; others say Elijah; and still others, Jeremiah or one of the prophets' (Matthew 16:14).

Despite the initial similarity in their summons to turn back to God 'for the forgiveness of sins' (Mark 1:4), Jesus went on to explain 'the good news of the kingdom' (Luke 4:43): God has given us power over sin, bringing freedom and new life for all who trust in him (e.g. Matthew 9:6; Mark 6:7; Luke 4:18, 36; John 5:24; 10:10). He embodied the 'true instruction' (or *true Law*) spoken of by Malachi that brings 'life and peace' and that would cause the Lord's name to 'be feared among the nations' (Malachi 2:5–6; 1:14). He also stressed the consequences for those who refuse to turn back to God: 'If anyone is ashamed of me and my words in this adulterous and sinful generation, the Son of Man will be ashamed of them when he comes in his Father's glory with the holy angels' (Mark 8:38).

It is worth asking why God needed John to prepare the people for the Messiah's coming. The answer is surely similar to why he continues to use his people today: to prepare others to encounter him. For the message of John was also the message of the twelve disciples (Mark 6:12) and of the early church (Acts 2:38). It remains the message of believers in every generation: 'Repent and believe in Jesus!' (see Acts 19:4).

As the very last word of the Old Testament significantly tells us, if John had not prepared the way for Jesus, then the Lord would have come and struck the earth with 'total destruction' – a *curse* (Malachi 4:6). That is why 'among those born of women there is no one greater than John' (Luke 7:28a). For John was the messenger who gave witness to the incarnate Jesus – God on earth – who 'redeemed us from the curse of the law by becoming a curse for us' (Galatians 3:13). That is also why 'the one who is least in the kingdom of God is greater than' John (Luke 7:28b). For *we* are the messengers who give witness to the *resurrected* Jesus: the God of justice who himself intervened to save us from death and to give us eternal life and peace – and who promised to come again (John

14:3). So, as Isaac Watts exhorts us in his carol 'Joy to the World': 'Let men their songs employ' – for 'the Saviour reigns' and 'He comes to make His blessings flow, far as the curse is found'.[2]

Pause to ponder
- How might a greater focus on the Incarnation help you and others to encounter Jesus and to enjoy his peace more deeply?
- How might a greater focus on the gospel of the kingdom, as taught by Jesus during his life on earth, also help you and others to encounter him more deeply?

---

2 Isaac Watts, 'Joy to the World, the Lord Is Come' (1719), Hymnary.org: https://hymnary.org/text/joy_to_the_world_the_lord_is_come (accessed 13 January 2024).

Day 15
The dreamer

This is how the birth of Jesus the Messiah came about: his mother Mary was pledged to be married to Joseph, but before they came together, she was found to be pregnant through the Holy Spirit. Because Joseph her husband was faithful to the law, and yet did not want to expose her to public disgrace, he had in mind to divorce her quietly.

But after he had considered this, an angel of the Lord appeared to him in a dream and said, 'Joseph son of David, do not be afraid to take Mary home as your wife, because what is conceived in her is from the Holy Spirit. She will give birth to a son, and you are to give him the name Jesus, because he will save his people from their sins.'

All this took place to fulfil what the Lord had said through the prophet: 'The virgin will conceive and give birth to a son, and they will call him Immanuel' (which means 'God with us').

When Joseph woke up, he did what the angel of the Lord had commanded him and took Mary home as his wife. But he did not consummate their marriage until she gave birth to a son. And he gave him the name Jesus.
(Matthew 1:18–25)

Quick glance

Matthew records that Joseph, the husband of Mary, has four life-changing dreams in the space of what was probably just a couple of years. In at least three of them an angel of the Lord appears to him. A distinctive feature of this portion of Scripture is how

Matthew repeatedly quotes passages of Old Testament prophecy and states that these have been fulfilled in Jesus. Only by recognising that Jesus fulfils the promises of many centuries will we truly comprehend who he is and how we should respond. In the past, God had spoken through his angels and prophets about things to come. Now, Joseph, by virtue of his relationship with Jesus – and the magi, by virtue of their faith in him – received messages that pertained to the here and now, ensuring the safety of the long-promised deliverer. We live in the days of which it was formerly promised: 'I will pour out my Spirit on all people. Your sons and daughters will prophesy, your old men will dream dreams, your young men will see visions.' This is where the wonder – the 'magic' – of Christmas begins.

In-depth reflection

Asked to name a character from the Bible who was known for their dreams, my guess is that most people would come up with Joseph, son of Jacob, made famous by the musical *Joseph and the Amazing Technicolor Dreamcoat* with its song 'Any Dream Will Do'.

The New Testament begins with 'the genealogy of Jesus the Messiah the son of David, the son of Abraham' (Matthew 1:1). This concludes with 'Jacob the father of Joseph, the husband of Mary, and Mary was the mother of Jesus who is called the Messiah' (Matthew 1:16). This Joseph son of Jacob would seem to have just as strong a claim to the title of dreamer as his namesake in Genesis.

After all, Matthew records that Joseph has four life-changing dreams in the space of what was probably just a couple of years. Now, I don't know if you have ever had a life-changing dream? Personally, I recall only having had one. That was when I awoke on Good Friday, 1991, and realised (as I noted on day 1) 'that, according to the standards of my own conscience, even I fell short of what might commonly be described as "good"'. Yet Joseph has four such dreams and in at least three of them an angel of the Lord appears to him.

Day 15

As a result of the first one, he takes Mary home as his wife. We know from Luke, who 'carefully investigated everything from the beginning' (Luke 1:3), that Mary lived in 'Nazareth, a town in Galilee' (Luke 1:26). We also know that she spent the first three months of her pregnancy with her relative Elizabeth in 'a town in the hill country of Judea' and then returned home (Luke 1:39, 56). Evidently, now that her pregnancy was becoming known, Joseph had the first of his dreams and dutifully took Mary home as his wife. Later, however, the couple 'went up from the town of Nazareth in Galilee to Judea, to Bethlehem the town of David' (Luke 2:4). A little later, we are told, 'while they were there, the time came for the baby to be born' (Luke 2:6). Forty days later, 'when the time came for the purification rites required by the Law of Moses', the family visited the Temple in Jerusalem (Luke 2:22). They then 'returned to Galilee to their own town of Nazareth' (Luke 2:39). So, the magi's visit to Bethlehem must have taken place in the first five weeks or so after Christ's birth.

For editorial reasons that we can never know, despite his careful investigations, Luke did not record the family's stay in Egypt. Most likely, it happened either before their presentation of Jesus in the Temple or else immediately afterwards. For Matthew connects their trip with the departure of the magi and Joseph's second dream:

> When [the magi] had gone, an angel of the Lord appeared to Joseph in a dream. 'Get up,' he said, 'take the child and his mother and escape to Egypt. Stay there until I tell you, for Herod is going to search for the child to kill him.'
> So he got up, took the child and his mother during the night and left for Egypt, where he stayed until the death of Herod.
> (Matthew 2:13–15)

Afterwards, Herod 'gave orders to kill all the boys in Bethlehem and its vicinity who were two years old and under' (Matthew 2:16). If Jesus and his family had already left the area, then they would have been safely out of harm's way in their own town of Nazareth, some 70 miles (110 km) from Bethlehem, as the crow flies. In which case, their flight to Egypt would seem to have been an unnecessary precaution.

Either way, it seems that they were not there for very long. For we also know that 'every year Jesus' parents went to Jerusalem for the Festival of the Passover' (Luke 2:41). In quick succession Joseph has his third and fourth dreams:

> After Herod died, an angel of the Lord appeared in a dream to Joseph in Egypt and said, 'Get up, take the child and his mother and go to the land of Israel, for those who were trying to take the child's life are dead.'
>
> So he got up, took the child and his mother and went to the land of Israel. But when he heard that Archelaus was reigning in Judea in place of his father Herod, he was afraid to go there. Having been warned in a dream, he withdrew to the district of Galilee, and he went and lived in a town called Nazareth. (Matthew 2:19–23)

The thing is: why did Matthew choose to begin his Gospel account in this way? What do we gain from his chapter-and-a-half record of the birth and early months of the life of Jesus? Why does Joseph have such a prominent role?

A distinctive feature of this portion of Scripture is how Matthew repeatedly quotes passages of Old Testament prophecy and states that these have been fulfilled in Jesus. This must be the key to answering our questions. Only by recognising that Jesus fulfils the promises of many centuries will we truly comprehend who he is and how we should respond.

Joseph's first dream leads to the conclusion from the prophet: '"The virgin will conceive and give birth to a son, and they will call him Immanuel" (which means "God with us")' (Matthew 1:23, quoting Isaiah 7:14). As we saw (on days 2 and 10), these words had an immediate fulfilment (in Isaiah 8) and the context was one of judgement and condemnation, the fall of two kingdoms:

Day 15

Hear now, you house of David! Is it not enough to try the patience of humans? Will you try the patience of my God also? Therefore the Lord himself will give you a sign: … before the boy knows enough to reject the wrong and choose the right, the land of the two kings you dread will be laid waste. The LORD will bring on you and on your people and on the house of your father a time unlike any since Ephraim broke away from Judah – he will bring the king of Assyria.
(Isaiah 7:13–17)

So a historic word of judgement is fulfilled; but, by means of the dream, God provides guidance that ensures the protection of the Christ.

The next dream in the sequence comes not to Joseph but to the magi: 'And having been warned in a dream not to go back to Herod, they returned to their country by another route' (Matthew 2:12). The prophecy quoted by Matthew in connection with this episode (in 2:6), foretelling that the ruler of God's people would come out of Bethlehem, comes before the dream. Its context is one not just of judgement but also of redemption:

Therefore Israel will be abandoned
　　until the time when she who is in labour bears a son,
and the rest of his brothers
　　return to join the Israelites.

He will stand and shepherd his flock
　　in the strength of the LORD,
　　in the majesty of the name of the LORD his God.
And they will live securely, for then his greatness
　　will reach to the ends of the earth …

I will take vengeance in anger and wrath
　　on the nations that have not obeyed me.
(Micah 5:3–4, 15)

Similarly, as we have seen already (on day 13), the context of the scripture that Matthew says was fulfilled in response to the third dream (Joseph's second) is one of restoration and hope. Yes, there will be 'weeping and great mourning' in Bethlehem. Nevertheless, God affirms: 'I am Israel's father, and Ephraim is my firstborn son' and comforts his people: 'Restrain your voice from weeping and your eyes from tears, for … there is hope for your descendants' (Jeremiah 31:9, 16–17).

In the past, God spoke through his angels and prophets of things to come. Through one of them, he promised: 'I will pour out my Spirit on all people. Your sons and daughters will prophesy, your old men will dream dreams, your young men will see visions' (Joel 2:28). Now, Joseph, by virtue of his relationship with Jesus – and the magi, by virtue of their faith in him – received messages that pertained to the here and now, ensuring the safety of the long-promised deliverer. As it is written, 'In the past God spoke to our ancestors through the prophets at many times and in various ways, but in these last days he has spoken to us by his Son' (Hebrews 1:1–2). As we saw previously (on day 13), the Lord had promised: 'No longer will they teach their neighbour, or say to one another, "Know the LORD," because they will all know me, from the least of them to the greatest' (Jeremiah 31:34). This is where the wonder – the 'magic' – of Christmas begins.

Pause to ponder
- How would you answer a friend who asks, 'How do you know if God's speaking to you?'
- In what ways has the Lord spoken to you during this past year – through circumstances, through your reading of Scripture, through other people or through dreams?

Day 16
The blessing

Praise be to the Lord, the God of Israel,
    because he has come to his people and redeemed them.
He has raised up a horn of salvation for us
    in the house of his servant David
(as he said through his holy prophets of long ago),
salvation from our enemies
    and from the hand of all who hate us –
to show mercy to our ancestors
    and to remember his holy covenant,
    the oath he swore to our father Abraham:
to rescue us from the hand of our enemies,
    and to enable us to serve him without fear
    in holiness and righteousness before him all our days.

And you, my child, will be called a prophet of the Most High;
    for you will go on before the Lord to prepare the way for him,
to give his people the knowledge of salvation
    through the forgiveness of their sins,
because of the tender mercy of our God,
    by which the rising sun will come to us from heaven
to shine on those living in darkness
    and in the shadow of death,
to guide our feet into the path of peace.
(Luke 1:68–79)

Quick glance

For Luke, the fulfilment of all the promises recorded in the Law of Moses and the Prophets begins with 'a priest named Zechariah'. What follows is a fulfilment of the prophetic pattern of miraculous births announced by a divine messenger. Zechariah himself also became a sign to the people. For his failure to believe the angel Gabriel was no different from Israel's failure to believe God's messengers in every generation. His period of silence and inability to speak emphasised the centuries between the Old and New Testaments when Israel heard no further word from the Lord. When this twofold silence is broken, Zechariah's prophetic blessing concerning his son's role contains two key elements: to prepare the way for the Lord; and 'to give his people the knowledge of salvation through the forgiveness of their sins'. These, as Luke will repeatedly remind us, are the key elements of our witness about Christ too, as we await his return. This is the Christmas blessing that we have received, the blessing for which we give thanks and the blessing that we are blessed to share with others!

In-depth reflection

As we saw yesterday, Matthew begins his Gospel with a clear statement that his account is about Jesus the Messiah. Even Mark, who (as we saw on day 14) starts with some background on John the Baptiser, commences with the words: 'The beginning of the good news about Jesus the Messiah …' (Mark 1:1). Not so Luke. Luke steps back even further. He writes 'an account of the things that have been fulfilled among us' (Luke 1:1). Jesus is not even mentioned in the first thirty verses. For Luke, the fulfilment of all those promises recorded in the Law of Moses and the Prophets begins not with Jesus; not with John; but with 'a priest named Zechariah' (Luke 1:5).

We first learn that Zechariah – John's father – 'belonged to the priestly division of Abijah' and 'his wife Elizabeth was also a descendant of Aaron' (Luke 1:5). This firmly establishes John's

Day 16

credentials as 'the messenger of the covenant' of Levi foretold by Malachi (on day 14).

Yet Luke's decision to begin his account of the good news with John's father is also highly symbolic. For 'once when Zechariah's division was on duty and he was serving as priest before God, he was chosen by lot, according to the custom of the priesthood, to go into the temple of the Lord and burn incense' (Luke 1:8–9). This was to be burned on 'the altar in front of the curtain that shields the ark of the covenant law – before the atonement cover that is over the tablets of the covenant law – where [the Lord would] meet with [Moses]' and his successors on behalf of God's people (Exodus 30:6). When the time came for Zechariah to burn the incense, 'an angel of the Lord' (identified in v. 19 as Gabriel) 'appeared to him, standing at the right side of the altar of incense' (Luke 1:11).

What follows is a fulfilment of the prophetic pattern of miraculous births that we previously considered (on day 2). As with Isaac, Samson and Samuel, a divine messenger announces the miraculous birth of a son to a childless couple – a couple said to be too old to conceive (Luke 1:36). As with Isaac, Samson and Samuel, Zechariah is given details about the mission of their promised son. As with Isaac, he is told what to name him. As with Samson and Samuel, he is also given additional requirements to follow. Samson's mother was instructed to abstain from wine. Samuel's mother was accused of being drunk but had abstained from alcohol. In John's case, he was 'never to take wine or other fermented drink' (Luke 1:15).

Luke had assured us that Zechariah and his wife 'were righteous in the sight of God, observing all the Lord's commands and decrees blamelessly' (Luke 1:6). Yet the priest fails to believe the angel's words or to recognise the historic pattern. Consequently, he is silenced and becomes unable to talk, being required to abstain from speaking until John's birth (Luke 1:20). Evidently, he is struck both deaf and dumb during this period, for his relatives later had to make signs to him, rather than just speak to him, 'to find out what he would like to name the child' (Luke 1:62).

Thus, Zechariah himself became a sign to the people. For his failure to believe Gabriel was no different from Israel's failure to believe God's messengers in every generation. His period of silence and inability to speak emphasised the centuries between the Old and New Testaments when Israel heard no further word from the Lord. Immediately after the promised messenger of the covenant was named, however, Zechariah's 'mouth was opened and his tongue set free, and he began to speak, praising God' – he was 'filled with the Holy Spirit and prophesied' (Luke 1:64, 67). The people of God would once again begin to hear from the Lord. More than that, the Lord would soon meet with his people again – and not just in the Temple, but in the person of Christ and, later, through the Holy Spirit!

The responses of Zechariah's wife Elizabeth are usually overlooked. Nevertheless, given that Luke was inspired to include them, they deserve our attention – all the more so because, like her husband, she too 'was filled with the Holy Spirit' (Luke 1:41). After she became pregnant, she acknowledged: 'The Lord has done this for me … In these days he has shown his favour and taken away my disgrace among the people' (Luke 1:25). Six months later, when Mary visits, Elizabeth exclaims with a great shout:

> Blessed are you among women, and blessed is the child you will bear! But why am I so favoured, that the mother of my Lord should come to me? As soon as the sound of your greeting reached my ears, the baby in my womb leaped for joy. Blessed is she who has believed that the Lord would fulfil his promises to her!
> (Luke 1:42–5)

The dominant theme here is clearly one of blessing. Two different words are actually used in the original Greek. The first is the kind of blessing associated with giving thanks; for example, before a meal (e.g. Luke 9:16; 24:30). The second is the kind associated with receiving favour; for example, as used by Jesus in the Beatitudes in his 'lesson on the mount' and 'lesson on the plain' (see Matthew 5:3–11; Luke 6:20–2), or when a subject is honoured to appear before a ruler (e.g. Acts 26:2). As yet, however, Elizabeth only

Day 16

recognises God's work in her own life and that of Mary. It will take her husband, who has nine months' aural and oral isolation to reflect on Gabriel's message, to identify the true significance of what is happening to them all.

Zechariah's prophetic praise starts off with a blessing 'to the Lord, the God of Israel'. This blessing, or *berakah*, is a traditional Jewish form of praise. In it the Lord is acknowledged as 'the God *of Israel*'. Its inspiration is Zechariah's recognition that the God of Israel has, as long promised, come and redeemed his people! This verse is ironically echoed in the mouths of the two disciples at the end of Luke's Gospel. While they travelled to Emmaus, they lamented that they 'had hoped that [Jesus] was the one who was going to redeem Israel' (Luke 24:21). They could not understand, even after the event, what Zechariah, being 'filled with the Holy Spirit', was able in advance to perceive, some six months before the Messiah was actually born. That is: through the Incarnation, God had redeemed his people.

Zechariah's blessing is very similar to Mary's earlier declaration of praise (Luke 1:46–55) in both its length and content. Mary begins by praising God for the news that the angel Gabriel has just given her. Three-fifths of her praise is then framed within the wider context of what God has done for all his people. She acknowledges that God has greater purposes for her miracle-born son. Zechariah includes a few words about his own son, but he dedicates more than four-fifths of his song to praise God for what he has done for his people. In addition, both of them twice mention God's mercy and refer to his promises to Abraham.

We previously observed (on day 8) how the responses of both Mary and Zechariah draw on the prayer of Hannah. As we recall, Hannah saw that the Lord would judge the ends of the earth (1 Samuel 2:10) and glimpsed that, somehow, the Anointed One was connected with the Lord's plans to reverse the fortunes of all. Mary also accepts that God 'has scattered those who are proud in their inmost thoughts' and that he has 'lifted up the humble' (Luke 1:51–2). Zechariah, however, sees even more clearly that salvation has come through 'the house of his servant David (as he said through

The blessing

his holy prophets of long ago)'. Incredibly, Zechariah comprehends that this salvation is based on the forgiveness of sins. This insight is clearly founded on the revelation of Isaiah that we saw (on day 11):

> Your iniquities have separated
>   you from your God;
> your sins have hidden his face from you,
>   so that he will not hear …
>
> The Redeemer will come to Zion,
>   to those in Jacob who repent of their sins …
> (Isaiah 59:2, 20)

Zechariah declares that the Lord has come to his people and will remove the thing that prevents us from having a relationship with him. As God revealed through Isaiah another time: 'I have swept away your offences like a cloud, your sins like the morning mist. Return to me, for I have redeemed you' (Isaiah 44:22). Again, a priest who had studied Isaiah would know that the Lord had declared, 'You were sold for nothing, and without money you will be redeemed' (Isaiah 52:3). The Lord has come to his people, Zechariah proclaims, enabling 'us to serve him without fear in holiness and righteousness before him all our days'.

Zechariah's prophetic blessing concerning his own son's role contains two key elements: to prepare the way for the Lord; and 'to give his people the knowledge of salvation through the forgiveness of their sins'. These, as we saw (on day 14) and as Luke will repeatedly remind us, are the key elements of our witness about Christ too, as we await his return:

- 'Repentance for the forgiveness of sins will be preached in his name to all nations, beginning at Jerusalem. You are witnesses of these things.' (Luke 24:47–8)
- 'Repent and be baptised, every one of you, in the name of Jesus Christ for the forgiveness of your sins. And you will receive the gift of the Holy Spirit. The promise is for you and your children

Day 16

and for all who are far off – for all whom the Lord our God will call.' (Acts 2:38–9)
- 'He commanded us to preach to the people and to testify that he is the one whom God appointed as judge of the living and the dead. All the prophets testify about him that everyone who believes in him receives forgiveness of sins through his name.' (Acts 10:42–3)
- 'Through Jesus the forgiveness of sins is proclaimed to you. Through him everyone who believes is set free from every sin.' (Acts 13:38–9)

This is the Christmas blessing that we have received, the blessing for which we give thanks and the blessing that we are blessed to share with others! Praise the Lord!

Pause to ponder
- Pray about who you could seek to talk with about this forgiveness in the coming day.
- How might you be able to include these ideas and maybe invite this person (or people) to a Christian event as you discuss your Christmas plans with them?

Day 17
The manger

And there were shepherds living out in the fields near by, keeping watch over their flocks at night. An angel of the Lord appeared to them, and the glory of the Lord shone around them, and they were terrified. But the angel said to them, 'Do not be afraid. I bring you good news that will cause great joy for all the people. Today in the town of David a Saviour has been born to you; he is the Messiah, the Lord. This will be a sign to you: you will find a baby wrapped in cloths and lying in a manger.'

Suddenly a great company of the heavenly host appeared with the angel, praising God and saying,

'Glory to God in the highest heaven,
    and on earth peace to those on whom his favour rests.'

When the angels had left them and gone into heaven, the shepherds said to one another, 'Let's go to Bethlehem and see this thing that has happened, which the Lord has told us about.'

So they hurried off and found Mary and Joseph, and the baby, who was lying in the manger. When they had seen him, they spread the word concerning what had been told them about this child, and all who heard it were amazed at what the shepherds said to them. But Mary treasured up all these things and pondered them in her heart. The shepherds returned, glorifying and praising God for all the things they had heard and seen, which were just as they had been told.
(Luke 2:8–20)

Quick glance

In the birth of Christ, Luke presents us with the ultimate fulfilment of the prophetic pattern of miraculous births announced by a divine messenger. As regards this long-promised miracle-born deliverer, we know that:

- God will establish an everlasting covenant with him;
- he will begin to save the people of God;
- he will preserve life for ever;
- he is the King of kings who will judge the nations;
- he will be 'separated to God' to complete our salvation – to save us once and for all;
- he will be anointed to reign on David's throne.

Jesus' nativity marks the culmination and fulfilment of all the promises of God throughout history – the beginning of a new era in our dealings with the Lord. So, like the owners of the manger, we too should welcome the Christ: not as a guest, on the periphery of our lives, but as the closest of family, into the heart of our homes and lives. We should join the angelic host and the shepherds in glorifying and praising God for all the marvellous things we have seen and heard.

In-depth reflection

How many times have you heard that Joseph and Mary were refugees? Or that the conditions into which Jesus was born were little better than a farmyard or zoo? Neither assertion, of course, finds any basis in Scripture. 'But', as people like to say, 'why let the truth ruin a good story?' Well, perhaps the truth is an even better story!

It is true, as we noted (on day 15), that Joseph and Mary travelled from their own town of Nazareth in Galilee up to Bethlehem in Judea while she was still expecting Jesus. There is, however, no sense of urgency regarding his birth. Rather, Luke simply states that 'while they were there, the time came for the baby to be born' (Luke 2:6).

It is also true that they were a poor family. After the birth, when they travelled to Jerusalem 'for the purification rites required by the Law of Moses', we are told that they offered 'a pair of doves or two young pigeons' (Luke 2:22–4). This, the Law tells us, is the regulation for a woman who gives birth but who 'cannot afford a lamb' (Leviticus 12:8).

It is not true, however, that they were strangers in a strange land. Far from it. Joseph 'belonged to the house and line of David' (Luke 2:4) and therefore had extensive family ties to Bethlehem. He was going back to the place of his roots. Mary also had relatives in the area. Just a few weeks or months earlier, she had visited her relative Elizabeth 'in the hill country of Judea' (Luke 1:39). We also know that twelve years later, when the family returned from their annual pilgrimage to Jerusalem, it was in a company of so many relatives and acquaintances that it took them a whole day to notice that they had left the boy Jesus behind (Luke 2:44). So, between them, they would have had plenty of relatives who would have welcomed them into their homes.

What, then, are we to make of the statement that 'there was no guest room available for them' (Luke 2:7)? First, the text makes no mention of an inn, as used by travellers, such as in the parable of the good Samaritan (Luke 10:34). Instead, Luke uses the same word that Jesus uses when he sends the disciples Peter and John ahead to prepare for the Passover. He tells them: 'Say to the owner of the house, "The Teacher asks: where is the *guest room*, where I may eat the Passover with my disciples?" He will show you a large room upstairs, all furnished. Make preparations there' (Luke 22:11–12).

We can find another example of such a guest room in the Old Testament. The prophet Elisha regularly stopped for a meal in the home of a well-to-do woman in a place called Shunem. One day, she said to her husband:

> I know that this man who often comes our way is a holy man of God. Let's make a small room on the roof and put in it a

Day 17

bed and a table, a chair and a lamp for him. Then he can stay there whenever he comes to us.
(2 Kings 4:9–10)

Another author writes of staying 'in just such a roof-room, jerry-built on the roof of a hotel in the Old City of Jerusalem, in the lee of the Jaffa Gate, in 1981'.[1] The same arrangement can still be found in villages and towns across the world today, notably in the Middle East and neighbouring regions. Even when I have stayed with relatively poor families in remote villages across Central Asia, the rooms of their homes have typically been arranged around a central courtyard. The guest room is separate from the family's main living quarters and has its own private entrance.

Luke begins his account of Jesus' birth by noting that the Roman authorities had decreed that a census be taken. As a result, 'everyone went to their own town to register' (Luke 2:3) and the town of David, which is called Bethlehem, would have been busy with extended families staying with relatives. Consequently, 'there was no place for them in the guest room' (Luke 2:7, literal translation). The guest room was packed with other visitors.

So what to do with an expectant relative soon to give birth? The same as you or I would do in similar circumstances – let alone what someone from a culture known for its generous hospitality would do – namely, invite them into our main living quarters. Yet Luke also tells us that Mary swaddled Jesus and laid him in a 'manger'. This is the same word used by Jesus when he rebukes a synagogue leader who had rebuked him for healing on the Sabbath: 'Doesn't each of you on the Sabbath untie your ox or donkey from the *stall* and lead it out to give it water?' (Luke 13:15).

Of course, I assume that you, like me, do not have an animal stall in your main living quarters. You and I, however, do not live in an average first-century Middle Eastern home. In many simple village homes, the room where animals were kept at night was connected

---

1 Ian Paul, 'Jesus Was Not Born in a Stable – and It Really Matters!', Psephizo, 24 November 2003: https://www.psephizo.com/biblical-studies/jesus-was-not-born-in-a-stable-and-it-really-matters (accessed 30 November 2023).

with the main living-room. The space where the family slept would often be on a raised platform, with the animal feeding stalls separating the two. This design ensures the safety of the livestock. It also allows the family to benefit from the warmth of the animals. A mid-nineteenth-century American missionary to the Middle East noted that such arrangements 'are still found in the dwellings of farmers in this region'.[2] An early twentieth-century German theologian who conducted extensive fieldwork concurred:

> In the East today the dwelling place of man and beast is often in one and the same room. It is quite the usual thing among the peasants for the family to live, eat, and sleep on a kind of raised terrace (Arab. *mastaba*) in the one room of the house, while the cattle, particularly the donkeys and oxen, have their place below on the actual floor (*ka' al-bet*) near the door.[3]

Similar arrangements could be found in twentieth-century eastern Europe:

> Though the single room of the house was scrubbed and polished, drifting across the room, permeating the walls and the fabric of the quilts was the acrid smell of the animals. The little pig stall was directly under the window by the door and its inhabitant lived practically as one of the family. It freely wandered into the house and out to the road near the house. The hens also were part of the family and came inside the house to lay their eggs by the stove and at night sat upon them there.[4]

---

2 William McClure Thomson, *The Land and the Book; or, Biblical illustrations drawn from the manners and customs, the scenes and scenery of the Holy Land* (New York, NY: Harper & Brothers, 1858), vol. 2, p. 503.

3 Gustaf Hermann Dalman, *Sacred Sites and Ways: Studies in the topography of the Gospels*, tr. Paul P. Levertoff (London: Society for Promoting Christian Knowledge, 1935), p. 41.

4 Marie Chapian, *Of Whom the World Was Not Worthy* (Minneapolis, MN; Bethany House, 1978), p. 27.

Day 17

A probable example of this can be seen in the book of Judges. Jephthah the Gileadite was a mighty warrior who made a vow to the Lord:

> If you give the Ammonites into my hands, whatever comes out of the door of my house to meet me when I return in triumph from the Ammonites will be the LORD's, and I will sacrifice it as a burnt offering.
> (Judges 11:30–1)

Clearly, he was expecting an animal to come out of his house. Yet that is not what happens:

> When Jephthah returned to his home in Mizpah, who should come out to meet him but his daughter, dancing to the sound of tambourines! She was an only child. Except for her he had neither son nor daughter. When he saw her, he tore his clothes and cried, 'Oh no, my daughter! You have brought me down and I am devastated. I have made a vow to the LORD that I cannot break.'
> (Judges 11:34–5)

Perhaps the book of Judges should be nicknamed the 'book of Fools'. For, as it wryly concludes, in those days 'everyone did as they saw fit' (Judges 21:25).

There is one last thing to observe about Luke's birth narrative. Disappointingly, even some of our greatest modern hymn writers continue to perpetuate the myth of a squalid stable, rather than celebrating, say, 'the manger of a humble dwelling'. Yet, if the conditions in Bethlehem had in any way resembled 'a lowly cattle-shed',[5] then the shepherds would undoubtedly have intervened. 'Come with us,' they would have protested; 'even we can do better than this!' This, however, is *not* what happened. Instead, they

---

[5] From the well-known carol 'Once in Royal David's City' (1848) by Cecil Frances Alexander.

The manger

'returned, glorifying and praising God for all they had heard and seen' (Luke 2:20).

Having cleared away the cobwebs of our traditions, we can now ask what difference all this makes. Rather than focusing on ideas that contradict what is recorded in the Bible, we can look to see what the author actually wrote. Through his account of the events surrounding John's birth (see day 16), Luke reminded us of the prophetic pattern of miraculous births. In the birth of Christ, he presents us with its ultimate fulfilment. Like Isaac, Samson and Samuel, a divine messenger announces the miraculous birth of a son to a childless couple – a couple who had not yet come together, for whom it was humanly impossible to conceive (Luke 1:34). As with Isaac, Mary is told what to name their baby. As with Isaac, Samson and Samuel, she is also given details about the mission of their promised son:

> He will be great and will be called the Son of the Most High. The Lord God will give him the throne of his father David, and he will reign over Jacob's descendants for ever; his kingdom will never end.
> (Luke 1:32–3)

So we should remind ourselves what else we know about this long-promised miracle-born deliverer:

- God would establish an everlasting covenant with him (day 2);
- he would begin to save the people of God (day 2);
- he would preserve life for ever (day 3);
- he is the King of kings who will judge the nations (day 5);
- he would be 'separated to God' to complete our salvation – to save us once and for all (day 7);
- he would be anointed to reign on David's throne (day 10).

No wonder, then, that after Jesus is born, his nativity is announced by yet another divine messenger! The fact that this angel is sent to a group of ordinary shepherds reinforces the simplicity of his birth.[6] Christ did not come 'robed in majesty and armed with strength' (Psalm 93:1). Instead, he was clothed with 'compassion, kindness, humility, gentleness and patience' (Colossians 3:12). He came for all. Perhaps in this episode we should also see an allusion to another of the prophets who wrote of the coming Messiah:

> 'I will place shepherds over them who will tend them, and they will no longer be afraid or terrified, nor will any be missing,' declares the LORD.
>
> > 'The days are coming,' declares the LORD,
> >   'when I will raise up for David a righteous Branch,
> > a King who will reign wisely
> >   and do what is just and right in the land.
> > In his days Judah will be saved
> >   and Israel will live in safety.
> > This is the name by which he will be called:
> >   The LORD Our Righteous Saviour.'
> > (Jeremiah 23:4–6)

Either way, after delivering his message of good news to the shepherds, the angel is joined by 'a great company of the heavenly host' praising God (Luke 2:13). Their chorus celebrates the culmination and fulfilment of all the promises of God throughout history. It recognises that Jesus' advent marks the beginning of a new era in our dealings with the Lord. So, like the owners of the manger, we too should welcome the Christ: not as a guest, on the periphery of our lives, but as the closest of family, into the heart of our homes and lives. We should join the angelic host and the shepherds in

---

[6] Contrary to the recent teaching of some, as David Croteau convincingly argues in his book *Urban Legends of the New Testament: 40 common misconceptions* (Nashville, TN: B&H Publishing Group, 2015), 'the biblical portrayal of a shepherd is extremely positive in the Old and New Testaments' (p. 19). If shepherds were despised in Israelite society, Joseph (son of the patriarch Jacob) would not have needed to explain to his family after their arrival in Egypt that 'all shepherds are detestable to the Egyptians' (Genesis 46:34).

The manger

glorifying and praising God for all the marvellous things we have seen and heard:

> Glory to God in the highest heaven,
>   and on earth peace to those on whom his favour rests.
> (Luke 2:14)

Pause to ponder

- How might reframing our view of the nativity to one rooted in the historical record, rather than on unsupported traditions, help us and the Church to rediscover the 'magic' of Christmas?
- From what areas of your life have you tended to exclude Christ? What would it mean to welcome him into those areas more fully?

Day 18
Glory, glory, alleluia!

There were shepherds living out in the fields near by, keeping watch over their flocks at night. An angel of the Lord appeared to them, and the glory of the Lord shone around them, and they were terrified. But the angel said to them, 'Do not be afraid. I bring you good news that will cause great joy for all the people. Today in the town of David a Saviour has been born to you; he is the Messiah, the Lord. This will be a sign to you: You will find a baby wrapped in cloths and lying in a manger.'

Suddenly a great company of the heavenly host appeared with the angel, praising God and saying,

'Glory to God in the highest heaven,
    and on earth peace to those on whom his favour rests.'
(Luke 2:8–14)

Quick glance

The 'great company of the heavenly host' (or 'army') praise God with the words, 'Glory in the highest to God, and on earth peace to people favoured.' The Old Testament word for 'glory' was used to convey a sense of importance or splendour and can often be translated 'wealth' or 'honour'. It is also used as an alternative way of talking about the 'vindication' and 'salvation' of God's people. Similarly, the New Testament word is sometimes contrasted with 'dishonour' and 'suffering'. There are only two passages in the Old Testament where glory and peace occur together. In both places, the context is the coming judgement of the Lord of Hosts. So the angelic army that appeared to the shepherds announces words of comfort and joy for God's people. Yet, implicitly, the angels also warn that the Lord will execute judgement on all people. Jesus links glory with judgement too. With good reason, then, in the last book of the Bible we read of an angel who proclaimed the eternal gospel: 'Fear God and give him *glory*, because the hour of his *judgment* has come.'

In-depth reflection

Most of us have our favourite Christmas carols. Luke records four songs of praise in connection with the birth of Christ. We could even call these the original Christmas carol collection. The first is the declaration of praise by Mary, mother of Jesus. As we saw (on day 8), this draws heavily on the prayer of Hannah, mother of the prophet Samuel. The second comes from the lips of Zechariah the priest who, after the birth of his son John the Baptiser, 'was filled with the Holy Spirit and prophesied' (Luke 1:67). As we saw (on day 16), this draws heavily not just on the prayer of Hannah but also on Isaiah. The third is sung by the angelic chorus that appeared to the shepherds. The last occurs when a man in the Temple called Simeon took the infant Jesus in his arms and praised God. Traditionally, these four songs of praise – or carols – are named after the first words in their Latin translations: the Magnificat, Benedictus, Gloria, and Nunc Dimittis.

Luke's four Christmas carols are closely related. The two chapters in which they occur are structured in a way that deliberately contrasts John and Jesus. So, to gain a better understanding of the carols, we should note this structure (see Table 5). The blocks with verse numbers highlighted in bold indicate where Luke has chosen to give greater emphasis to one of the two main characters.

Even before we are told about their adult lives, Luke clearly signals that the Lord Jesus is greater than his messenger John:

- He provides us with far more historical detail relating to the circumstances of Jesus' birth than he does for John. This is

Day 18

Table 5 The contrast between John and Jesus in Luke chapters 1 and 2

1:5–23	Annunciation of John's birth	1:26–37	Annunciation of Jesus' birth
1:24–5	Response of John's mother	1:38	Response of Jesus' mother
1:39–56	Parallel greeting of mothers and unborn children Blessing by Elizabeth → Magnificat by Mary		
1:57	Birth of John	2:1–7	Birth of Jesus
1:58	Neighbours and relatives share parents' joy	2:8–20	Shepherds and angels share parents' joy → Gloria
1:59–66	Circumcision and naming of John	2:21	Circumcision and naming of Jesus
1:67–79	Prophetic greeting of John by an old man[1] who embodies the piety of Israel → Benedictus	2:22–35	Prophetic greeting of Jesus by an old man[2] who embodies the piety of Israel → Nunc Dimittis
		2:36–9	Prophetic greeting of Jesus by an old woman who embodies the piety of Israel
1:80	Growth of child	2:40	Growth of child
		2:41–52	Superior growth of Jesus in extra temple scene

fitting as the birth of Christ is the most miraculous of all, given that his mother had 'known no man' (Luke 1:34, literal translation).

- The neighbours and relatives who share in the parents' joy include outsiders 'living out in the fields near by' and 'a great company of the heavenly host' who praise God (Luke 2:8, 13).
- Not just one but two prophetic witnesses in the Temple speak of the redemption and salvation that Jesus brings.

---

1 Zechariah is described as 'very old' (Luke 1:7), although, as he was serving in the Temple, we know that he had not yet reached the priestly retirement age of 50 (Numbers 8:25).
2 In contrast with the prophet Anna, we are not actually told the age of Simeon. It is traditionally assumed that he was also old on the basis that 'it had been revealed to him by the Holy Spirit that he would not die before he had seen the Lord's Messiah' (Luke 2:26). We know too, however, that sometimes 'the righteous are taken away to be spared from evil' (Isaiah 57:1), leaving 'the wicked living long in their wickedness' (Ecclesiastes 7:15).

- Whereas John 'became strong in spirit' (Luke 1:80), we are twice told that Jesus grew in wisdom and grace (or favour). As a growing child, Jesus came again to the Temple, where 'everyone who heard him was amazed at his understanding and his answers' (Luke 2:47).

The only area in which Luke focuses greater attention on John is over the circumcision and naming. As we saw (on day 16), this serves to highlight John's role as 'prophet of the Most High' (Luke 1:76). In terms of its function within the structure of the text, Zechariah's carol parallels Simeon's much shorter one. Both share the same central theme: God's salvation. In length, however, Simeon's carol more closely resembles that of the angels. So it is worth considering these together.

The 'great company of the heavenly host' (or 'army') praise God with the words, 'Glory in the highest to God, and on earth peace to people favoured' (Luke 2:14, literal translation). This is very similar to the praise of the crowd of disciples when Jesus approached Jerusalem at the end of his life: 'Peace in heaven and glory in the highest!' (Luke 19:38).

Yet what is this 'glory'? It is not a word that most people use in normal conversation. In the Old Testament, the word used means 'weight' or 'heaviness'. It was used to convey a sense of importance or splendour and can often be translated 'wealth' or 'honour'. For instance, it is first used to speak of Jacob, when Laban's sons complained: 'Jacob has taken everything our father owned and has gained all this *wealth* from what belonged to our father' (Genesis 31:1). Later, it is used of his son Joseph, who tells his brothers: 'Tell my father about all the *honour* accorded me in Egypt and about everything you have seen' (Genesis 45:13). Used of God, the psalmist wrote: 'The heavens declare the *glory* of God; the skies proclaim the work of his hands' (Psalm 19:1). When Isaiah saw a vision of the Lord, the fiery angels surrounding his throne were calling to one another: 'Holy, holy, holy is the LORD Almighty; the whole earth is full of his *glory*' (Isaiah 6:3).

Day 18

The word is also used as an alternative way of talking about the 'vindication' and 'salvation' of God's people. Significantly, this is in the broader context of the coming Saviour and his promised redemption:

> For Zion's sake I will not keep silent,
>   for Jerusalem's sake I will not remain quiet,
> till her *vindication* shines out like the dawn,
>   her *salvation* like a blazing torch.
> The nations will see your *vindication*,
>   and all kings your *glory*;
> you will be called by a new name
>   that the mouth of the LORD will bestow ...
>
> The LORD has made proclamation
>   to the ends of the earth:
> 'Say to Daughter Zion,
>   "See, your Saviour comes!
> See, his reward is with him,
>   and his recompense accompanies him."'
> They will be called the Holy People,
>   the Redeemed of the LORD;
> and you will be called Sought After,
>   the City No Longer Deserted.
> (Isaiah 62:1–2, 11–12)

We find the same range of meaning in the Greek word used for glory in the New Testament. So, at one end, Jesus taught: 'Consider how the wild flowers grow. They do not labour or spin. Yet I tell you, not even Solomon in all his *splendour* was dressed like one of these' (Luke 12:27). Later, when Paul described the light that flashed around him on the road to Damascus, he said: 'My companions led me by the hand into Damascus, because the *brilliance* of the light had blinded me' (Acts 22:11).

At the other end of the word's range, in his letters to the churches, Paul contrasts glory with dishonour and suffering. Thus, regarding the resurrection of the dead, using the metaphor of a seed for the natural body, he writes: 'it is sown in <u>dishonour</u>, it is raised in *glory*; it is sown in <u>weakness</u>, it is raised in *power*' (1 Corinthians 15:43). He also contrasts our 'momentary, light <u>troubles</u>' with 'an eternal weight of *glory*' (2 Corinthians 4:17, personal translation). Jesus himself also highlighted this connection between glory and suffering. Appearing to two of the disciples after his resurrection, he asked: 'Did not the Messiah have to <u>suffer</u> these things and then enter his *glory*?' (Luke 24:26).[3]

There are only two passages in the Old Testament where glory and peace occur together. The first is at the end of Isaiah, where the Lord summarises his twin message of comfort and judgement. Appropriately, the setting is that of a mother nursing an infant child:

[God says:] 'Rejoice with Jerusalem, and be glad for her,
    all you who love her;
rejoice with her in joy,
    all you who mourn over her;
that you may nurse and be satisfied
    from her consoling breast;
that you may drink deeply with delight
    from her glorious abundance.'
For thus says the LORD:
'Behold, I will extend **peace** to her like a river,
    and the *glory* of the nations like an overflowing stream;
and you shall nurse, you shall be carried upon her hip,
    and bounced upon her knees.
As one whom his mother comforts,
    so I will comfort you;
    you shall be comforted in Jerusalem.'
(Isaiah 66:10–13 ESV)

---

[3] For further examples where glory is contrasted with suffering, see Romans 2:9–10; 8:18; Ephesians 3:13; Hebrews 2:10; 1 Peter 1:11; 4:13.

Day 18

The passage continues with an allusion to the heavenly hosts, warning that the Lord is coming with his chariots and his sword: 'the Lord will execute judgment on all people, and many will be those slain by the Lord' (Isaiah 66:15–16). The other place featuring both glory and peace is in another of the prophets. Like the angels in Luke 2:14, this also references the heavens and the earth:

> This is what the Lord Almighty says: 'In a little while I will once more shake the **heavens** and the **earth**, the sea and the dry land. I will shake all nations, and what is desired by all nations will come, and I will fill this house with *glory*,' says the Lord Almighty. 'The silver is mine and the gold is mine,' declares the Lord Almighty. 'The *glory* of this present house will be greater than the *glory* of the former house,' says the Lord Almighty. 'And in this place I will grant **peace**,' declares the Lord Almighty.
> (Haggai 2:6–9)

Haggai, like Isaiah, presents a message of hope for God's people. Like Isaiah, he also does so in the context of the Lord's coming judgement of all nations. He is more explicit than Isaiah, however, that God is the 'Lord Almighty' – or, more literally, 'the Lord of Hosts'. So yes, the angelic army that appeared to the shepherds revealed that the Messiah – the one 'desired by all nations' – had come. To those who 'feared a mega fear' (Luke 2:9, literal translation), they announced words of comfort and 'mega joy' for God's people: 'peace to those on whom his favour rests'. Yet, implicitly, they also warned that the Lord 'will execute judgment on all people' when he shakes the nations.

Jesus links glory with judgement too. He contrasts the Son of Man's 'throne of *glory*' with the 'twelve thrones' on which his followers will sit 'judging the twelve tribes of Israel' (Matthew 19:28, personal translation). In another place he says: 'I am not seeking *glory* for myself; but there is one who seeks it, and he is the judge' (John 8:50). In the last book of the Bible we even learn of an angel:

Glory, glory, alleluia!

> He had the eternal gospel to proclaim to those who live on the earth – to every nation, tribe, language and people. He said in a loud voice, 'Fear God and give him *glory*, because the hour of his judgment has come.'
> (Revelation 14:6–7)

Sadly, beside one modern Christmas song that dares to mention the choice we must each make between heaven and hell, the closest most carols come to reflecting on these themes is Edmund Sears's 'It Came Upon the Midnight Clear' with its description of the angels as they await the second advent of Christ:

> Still through the cloven skies they come
> with peaceful wings unfurled,
> and still their heavenly music floats
> o'er all the weary world;
> above its sad and lowly plains,
> they bend on hovering wing,
> and ever o'er its Babel sounds
> the blessed angels sing.
>
> And ye, beneath life's crushing load,
> whose forms are bending low,
> who toil along the climbing way
> with painful steps and slow,
> look now! for glad and golden hours
> come swiftly on the wing.
> O rest beside the weary road,
> and hear the angels sing![4]

Pause to ponder
- How does this broader sense of 'glory' provide a different perspective on your present sufferings and troubles?

---

[4] From 'It Came upon the Midnight Clear' (1849) by Edmund Sears, Hymnary.org: https://hymnary.org/text/it_came_upon_the_midnight_clear (accessed 7 March 2022).

Day 18

- Why do you think justice and judgement do not feature more often in our Christmas carols? Perhaps try to write an extra verse to one of your favourites!

Day 19
Purification and praise

When the parents brought in the child Jesus to do for him what the custom of the Law required, Simeon took him in his arms and praised God, saying:

> 'Sovereign Lord, as you have promised,
>   you may now dismiss your servant in peace.
> For my eyes have seen your salvation,
>   which you have prepared in the sight of all nations:
> a light for revelation to the Gentiles,
>   and the glory of your people Israel.'

The child's father and mother marvelled at what was said about him. Then Simeon blessed them and said to Mary, his mother: 'This child is destined to cause the falling and rising of many in Israel, and to be a sign that will be spoken against, so that the thoughts of many hearts will be revealed. And a sword will pierce your own soul too.'
(Luke 2:27–35)

Quick glance

Simeon's praise begins by stressing that the long-awaited fulfilment of God's promises has finally arrived. Dramatically, he asserts that the non-Jewish peoples will have a share in God's great salvation too. The prophet Anna also 'spoke about the child to all who were looking forward to the redemption of Jerusalem'. No doubt both of them would have been conscious that God's redemption had always been accompanied by judgement. Zechariah also informed us that the promised 'horn of salvation' would guide us into 'the way of peace'. When we next see the Lord in the Temple, he is aged 12. For three days his parents cannot find him. The word used to describe the anguish of their separation is the same as that felt by the rich man in Jesus' parable who begged Abraham to send the beggar Lazarus to relieve his thirst in Hades. So too will it be at Christ's return for those separated from the Lord because they refused to let his light guide them from the shadow of death into his path of peace and everlasting life.

In-depth reflection

Like the shepherds, we must hasten on. We saw (on day 17) that Joseph and Mary took Jesus 'to Jerusalem to present him to the Lord (as it is written in the Law of the Lord, "Every firstborn male is to be consecrated to the Lord")' (Luke 2:22–3). Prior to this, we are also told that 'on the eighth day, when it was time to circumcise the child, he was named Jesus, the name the angel had given him before he was conceived' (Luke 2:21). All this might seem oddly unnecessary to us. After all, thirty years later, 'Jesus came from Galilee to the Jordan to be baptised by John. But John tried to deter him, saying, "I need to be baptised by you, and do you come to me?"' (Matthew 3:13–14).

We might also think that there was no need for the Messiah to submit himself to the requirements of either God's covenant with Abraham or the Law – that is, circumcision and consecration (as recorded in Genesis 17:9–14 and Exodus 13:2, respectively). Yet it was proper for Jesus to undergo these rituals. For circumcision and consecration were outward signs of God's covenant promises to his people. As Jesus replied to John, 'Let it be so now; it is proper for us to do this to fulfil all righteousness' (Matthew 3:15). Abraham, too, we are told 'received circumcision as a sign, a seal of the righteousness that he had by faith while he was still uncircumcised' (Romans 4:11).

Today, baptism and taking communion bear witness to what God has *already* done in the lives of believers. So, too, circumcision

Purification and praise

and consecration did not bring about change. Rather, they pointed to the existing relationship between God and his people. Jesus later taught that he had not 'come to abolish the Law or the Prophets … but to fulfil them' (Matthew 5:17). In Christ, then, God's promises were both affirmed and realised.

Thus we meet Simeon in the Temple, a 'righteous and devout' man who 'was waiting for the consolation of Israel' (Luke 2:25). His greeting parallels Jacob's words of praise in Egypt on seeing his lost son Joseph (the original dreamer): 'Now I am ready to die, since I have seen for myself that you are still alive' (Genesis 46:30). 'Moved by the Spirit', Simeon's praise begins (in the original Greek) with an emphatic 'Now'. This stresses that the long-awaited fulfilment of God's promises has finally arrived. Through Christ, the time of salvation has *now* come. More than that, in the person of Jesus, whose name means 'The Lord Is Salvation', salvation has come.

Addressing God as 'Sovereign Lord' – or 'Master' – Simeon declares that he has seen the Lord's salvation. He uses an unusual form of the word 'salvation' that appears just five times in the New Testament. Its use in Luke 3:6, Acts 28:28 and Titus 2:11 makes explicit that the word is reminiscent of Isaiah 52:10: 'all the ends of the earth will see the salvation of our God.' It does not apply just to Israel but is universally inclusive. As Simeon declares, God prepared this salvation 'before the face of *all the peoples*' (Luke 2:31, literal translation). All of the prophecies and promises throughout history, he recognises, have *now* been fulfilled. As Paul later insists, 'I tell you, *now* is the time of God's favour, *now* is the day of salvation' (2 Corinthians 6:2). The Lord has come as 'a light for revelation to the Gentiles, and the glory of your people Israel'.

Thus, Simeon's carol picks up the themes of Zechariah's and Mary's carols. Namely, God has acted decisively to save his people, and this salvation is rooted in his dealings with Israel. Dramatically, though, Simeon also asserts that the non-Jewish peoples will have a share in God's great salvation too. As Isaiah revealed (on day 10), the new light that God planned would dawn over the peoples of *all* the nations.

Day 19

We come next to the second prophetic greeting of Jesus by an elderly worshipper who embodies the piety of Israel. Strikingly, this prophet has the same name (in Greek) as Samuel's mother Hannah, who also 'worshipped night and day, fasting and praying' in the Temple (Luke 2:37). Although we are not told what the prophet Anna said, we know that she also 'spoke about the child to all who were looking forward to the redemption of Jerusalem' (Luke 2:38). The word 'redemption' only occurs twice elsewhere in the New Testament: once in Hebrews 9:12 and once in Luke's parallel text, at the start of Zechariah's carol.

John's father invited praise to the Lord 'because he has come to his people and redeemed them' (Luke 1:68). Perhaps he drew inspiration from the Old Testament songs: 'He provided redemption for his people; he ordained his covenant for ever – holy and awesome is his name' (Psalm 111:9). Zechariah concluded his praise by linking our Redeemer's mission with the theme of light and darkness that we have already noted several times (on days 8 to 11): 'the rising sun will come to us from heaven to shine on those living in darkness and in the shadow of death'. This too draws on insights recorded in Isaiah, where the prophet said that the purpose of the Servant of the Lord was 'to open eyes that are blind, to free captives from prison and to release from the dungeon those who sit in darkness' (Isaiah 42:7). He was to declare 'to those in darkness, "Be free!"' (Isaiah 49:9). No doubt both Zechariah and Anna would have been conscious that God's redemption had always been accompanied by judgement too. As the Lord told Moses in Egypt, when he promised to free the Israelites: 'I will redeem you with an outstretched arm and with mighty acts of judgment' (Exodus 6:6).

Zechariah also informs us what this 'rising sun' that comes to us from heaven will achieve. By shining on those who live in the shadow of death, it will 'guide our feet into the path of peace'. The promised 'horn of salvation' (Luke 1:69) – now raised up (or, brought into existence) – will guide us into 'the way of peace' (v. 79 ESV). This is a phrase from Isaiah 59:8, where it is twinned (as we saw on day 11) with paths of justice. This path is no less than the way that was mapped out throughout the Law of Moses and

Purification and praise

the Prophets: 'keep the *way* of the LORD by doing what is right and *just*, so that the LORD will bring about for Abraham what he has promised him' (Genesis 18:19). It is the path that, by faith, was followed by the fathers of Israel – by Abraham, Moses, Joshua and David, who knew that 'all his *ways* are *just*' (Deuteronomy 32:4). It is the path foreseen by the prophets: 'I will lead the blind by *ways* they have not known, along unfamiliar *paths* I will guide them; I will turn the *darkness* into *light* before them and make the rough places smooth' (Isaiah 42:16).

So the salvation and redemption that came with Christ's birth are a continuation of God's former covenant mercy. The intention is that we might 'serve [God] without fear in holiness and righteousness before him all our days' (Luke 1:74–5). Although we claim this for ourselves as individuals, we do so in the context of the community of all God's people. This is a community founded on the history and culture of the seed of Abraham, the family of Isaac and the nation of David. As presented by Luke – that is, by Mary, Zechariah, the angels, Simeon and Anna – the Gentile nations are not saved *apart from* Israel. Rather, we are redeemed *as part of* the true Israel. Along with the 'many thousands of Jews' who believe and are 'zealous for the law', as reported in the early church (Acts 21:20), the true people of God consists of 'persons from every tribe and language and people and nation' (Revelation 5:9).

Having spotted these patterns, what difference would it make if Luke had not included the four songs of praise? The end of the first section (Luke 1:5–56) would instead conclude with Elizabeth's blessing of Mary. There would be no parallel prophetic section in connection with John. The angels would still announce their good news to the shepherds, but there would be no overtones of judgement. Lastly, Simeon would still bless and prophesy over Jesus and his parents, but the text would not include the Gentile nations. Without the four carols, we would lose all these insights from the Old Testament that Mary, Zechariah, the angels, Simeon and Anna together share with us.

Before we move on, there remains a vital part of Simeon's message to which we have not yet given attention. He warned that 'this child is destined to cause the falling' as well as the 'rising [or literally, "resurrection"] of many in Israel' (Luke 2:34). He also cautioned Mary: 'a sword will pierce your own soul too' (Luke 2:35). When we next see the Lord coming to the Temple, it is at the time of Passover. Now aged 12, for three days Jesus cannot be found by those who love him (Luke 2:46). The word used to describe the anguish of separation that his parents felt during these three days is the same as that felt by the rich man in Jesus' parable who begged Abraham to send the beggar Lazarus to relieve his thirst in Hades (Luke 16:24–5). So too will it be at Christ's return for those who find themselves separated from the Lord because they refused to let his light guide them from the shadow of death into his path of peace – a path that leads to everlasting life.

Given the undertones of judgement that we discerned in the songs inspired by Christ's birth, these three days seem to foreshadow the end of his life on earth. For, after his crucifixion, Jesus would again be absent for three days. As the downcast disciples on the Emmaus road observed, 'it is the third day since all this took place'. As yet, they had not realised that their new travelling companion was the one who they had hoped 'was going to redeem Israel' (Luke 24:21). Most people will hear and sing carols telling the news of Christ's birth this season. Not all, however, will recognise him as the one that can satisfy all their hopes. So, as Jesus repeatedly said, 'Whoever has ears to hear, let them hear' (Luke 8:8; 14:35).

Pause to ponder
- For which friends, family members or colleagues would you feel most anguish if they were to miss out on the Lord's path of peace and everlasting life?
- How might you prayerfully seek specific opportunities to talk with these individuals about God's salvation or to invite them to a Christmas celebration in the coming week?

Day 20
God's dwelling-place

In the beginning was the Word, and the Word was with God, and the Word was God. He was with God in the beginning. Through him all things were made; without him nothing was made that has been made. In him was life, and that life was the light of all mankind. The light shines in the darkness, and the darkness has not overcome it.

There was a man sent from God whose name was John. He came as a witness to testify concerning that light, so that through him all might believe. He himself was not the light; he came only as a witness to the light.

The true light that gives light to everyone was coming into the world. He was in the world, and though the world was made through him, the world did not recognise him. He came to that which was his own, but his own did not receive him. Yet to all who did receive him, to those who believed in his name, he gave the right to become children of God – children born not of natural descent, nor of human decision or a husband's will, but born of God.

The Word became flesh and made his dwelling among us. We have seen his glory, the glory of the one and only Son, who came from the Father, full of grace and truth.
(John 1:1–14)

Quick glance

The physical gathering of God's people is, to quote one writer, 'a revolutionary act' because so was the Incarnation itself. The presence of God among humankind was so world-shattering

Day 20

because, by it, 'Man has been recreated'. John's Gospel begins by intricately bringing together the ideas of John the Baptiser's testimony and God dwelling among us. The glory of this new 'dwelling' is far greater than that of Solomon's 'house'. Yet it is also tinged with a hint of judgement. So Christmas presents us all with a choice. Remarkably, if we receive Christ as the one in whom is life and true enlightenment, then we ourselves are God's dwelling-place. It is now us – the family of believers, regularly gathering together as the assembly of God's children – who serve as 'a witness to testify concerning that light' so that through us 'all might believe'. This is 'the incarnational reality' of what it means to be a follower of Christ – and to live human life to the full – 'if indeed we share in his sufferings in order that we may also share in his glory'.

In-depth reflection

In an article entitled 'The Local Church as a Counterculture', Brett McCracken (the senior editor at the Gospel Coalition) commented on *'the crucial physicality of the church* as the "body of Christ" in the material not just theoretical sense':

> The church's physical gathering in a common space for a few hours on a Sunday is a revolutionary act. We need to recognise what a countercultural gift this is. Churches today should emphasize the physicality of worship and liturgy, the practice of the Lord's Supper, passing the peace, bodily movement in worship, shaking hands and hugging each other – anything to remind their congregations that we are here, together, in the presence of God. One of the greatest gifts of the 21st-century church will be to re-sensitize people to the incarnational reality of what it means to be human.[1]

---

1 Brett McCracken, 'The Local Church as a Counterculture', 9Marks, 17 April 2018: https://www.9marks.org/article/the-local-church-as-a-counterculture (accessed 19 March 2022); my emphasis.

It is worth noting that he wrote these words in 2018 – before the restrictions of what some dubbed the 'post-freedom era' or 'Covid era'. Most churches seemed to accept the constantly changing constraints on their ability to worship together and reach out to their communities without stopping to ask whether they should question them. Few churches preached on the Bible's most frequent command, 'Do not fear', to balance their exhortations to 'submit to the authorities' (Romans 13:5). Even fewer asked to what extent they should 'obey God rather than human beings' (Acts 5:29).

Churches that remained open despite state mandates, such as John MacArthur's Grace Community Church in southern California, were newsworthy because they were so few. Yet, as Capitol Hill Baptist Church successfully maintained in the District of Columbia, 'It is for the Church, not the District or this Court, to define for itself the meaning of "not forsaking the assembling of ourselves together." Hebrews 10:25.'[2] In the UK, it was several months before church leaders organised themselves to lodge a protest against 'policies which prioritise bare existence at the expense of those things that give quality, meaning and purpose to life' and to argue that 'regular gathering to worship God is essential for human life to be lived to the full'.[3] In the words of the medieval theologian Remigio de' Girolami, 'If he is not a citizen, he is not a man.'[4] By extension, we might add: if a person is not a citizen of heaven – and therefore actively involved in the community of God's people – they are not fully the individual that God created them to be.

What does this have to do with Christmas, you might well ask. Why introduce politics so close to Christmas? In short, because that is precisely what John does in the opening to his Gospel

---

[2] Jeff Pickering, 'Update: Capitol Hill Baptist Wins in District Court', The Ethics and Religious Liberty Commission of the Southern Baptist Convention, 10 October 2020: https://erlc.com/resource-library/articles/update-capitol-hill-baptist-wins-in-district-court (accessed 19 March 2022).

[3] 'Pastors Plead with UK's Leaders Not to Shut Down Churches Again', Christian Today, 22 September 2020: https://www.christiantoday.com/article/pastors.plead.with.uks.leaders.not.to.shut.down.churches.again/135608.htm (accessed 19 March 2022).

[4] Quoted in Rory Cox, *John Wyclif on War and Peace*, Royal Historical Society Studies in History (Woodbridge: Boydell Press, 2014), p. 114.

account! When 'the Word became flesh', our world was instantly and for ever transformed. The physical gathering of God's people is, in the words of Brett McCracken, 'a revolutionary act' because so was the Incarnation itself. Not just in the sense of 'radical change', but also because it was quite literally a 'return to its starting point'[5] or a 'return to its origins'.[6] The presence of God among humankind was so world-shattering because, by it, 'Man has been recreated'.[7] Now, 'the manhood of Christ is the basis of the manhood of every individual'.[8] In the words of a former bishop of Lincoln, Robert Grosseteste, the Incarnation was the 'final act in the unfolding drama of creation: it made Man and Nature complete, and it bound the whole created universe together in union with God'.[9] That is, 'The incarnation of Christ completed God's creation.'[10] In fact, it was 'the divine purpose conceived before the beginning of created beings ... the preconceived goal for which everything exists'.[11] By it, God showed us how and what it means to be fully human. In order to unlock why this is so, we need to note two unusual features in John's account of the good news of Jesus.

---

5   David Como, 'God's Revolutions: England, Europe, and the concept of revolution in the mid-seventeenth century', in Keith Michael Baker and Dan Edelstein (eds), *Scripting Revolution: A historical approach to the comparative study of revolutions* (Stanford, CA: Stanford University Press, 2015), p. 44.

6   Louis Salleron, *La Nouvelle Messe*, 2nd edn (Paris: Nouvelles éditions latines, 1976), p. 40: 'dans les sociétés établies, un procédé révolutionnaire éprouvé est le retour aux origines' ('in established societies, a proven revolutionary process is the return to the origins').

7   Morna Hooker, *From Adam to Christ: Essays on Paul*, 2nd edn (Eugene, OR: Wipf & Stock, 2008), p. 23.

8   Herbert Workman, *John Wyclif: A study of the English medieval Church* (Oxford: Clarendon Press, 1926), vol. 1, p. 139.

9   Robert Grosseteste (*c.* 1235), quoted in Stephen Lahey, 'Wyclif's Trinitarian and Christological Theology', in *A Companion to John Wyclif: Late medieval theologian* (Leiden: Brill, 2006), p. 169.

10 Cox, *John Wyclif on War and Peace*, p. 132. See also Stephen Need, *The Gospels Today: Challenging readings of John, Mark, Luke & Matthew* (Lanham, MD: Cowley Publications, 2007): 'The incarnation in Jesus is not the sudden arrival of an otherwise absent Logos, but rather the completion of a process already begun in God's act of creation' (p. 13, ch. 1, 'Rereading the Prologue: Incarnation and Creation in John 1.1–18').

11 Maximus Confessor, *Questions and Responses for Thalassius* 60, quoted in Paul Blowers, *Maximus the Confessor: Jesus Christ and the transfiguration of the world* (Oxford: Oxford University Press, 2016), p. 106.

God's dwelling-place

First, in a deliberate echo of the first book of the Bible, John starts his Gospel before the creation of space and time: 'In the beginning'. He explicitly locates Christ's origins in the eternal realm outside history: 'He was with God in the beginning.' More than that, John insists that 'the Word was God', that 'through him all things were made' and that 'without him nothing was made that has been made'.[12] In a further allusion to Genesis, he is described as 'the true light that gives light to everyone'. To conclude his introduction, John notes: 'No one has ever seen God, but the one and only Son, who is himself God and is in the closest relationship with the Father, has made him known' (John 1:18).

Strangely, twice in the course of this short biography of Jesus, John interrupts himself to tell us about 'a man sent from God whose name was John' – namely, the Baptiser. The first time, in verses 6–8, we are told that this man 'came as a witness to testify concerning that light, so that through him all might believe'. The second time, in verse 15, we are presented with a somewhat opaque line of his testimony about the one 'who comes after me' yet who also 'was before me'. John then follows this interrupted portrait of Jesus with three further records, in verses 19–36, of John's testimony about Christ. In all, twenty-two of the chapter's first thirty-six verses are about John the Baptiser, rather than about the main character, Jesus.

So the first of the two unusual features in this fourth Gospel is the centrality of John as the messenger who bore witness to the incarnate Jesus as God on earth. As we saw (on day 14), this points to the way in which we are now the messengers who continue to bear witness to the resurrected Jesus.

The second unusual feature is the curious expression 'The Word became flesh and made his dwelling among us' (John 1:14). The word translated 'made his dwelling' has its root in the word for 'tent'. So God is depicted as pitching his tent among us. The verb

---

12 'Christ's mediation of creation is not to be thought of primarily in terms of the temporal beginning of the world. It is rather to be understood in terms of the whole of the world process that receives its unity and meaning in the light of its end that has appeared in advance in the history of Jesus.' Wolfhart Pannenberg, *Jesus – God and Man*, 2nd ed. (Croydon: SCM Classics, 2002), p. 391.

Day 20

only occurs four other times in the New Testament, each time in Revelation. When it is used with the same preposition, 'among', it refers to 'those who dwell in heaven' (Revelation 12:12; 13:6 ESV). Ultimately, God has dwelt with us on earth in order that we might dwell with him in heaven.

The full significance of the word is to be found in the Old Testament. In times past, the Levites 'ministered with music before the *tabernacle*, the *tent of meeting*, until Solomon built the *temple* of the LORD in Jerusalem' (1 Chronicles 6:32). The words for 'tabernacle' and 'temple' are, literally, 'dwelling-place' and 'house'. This was the place where God's people were able to meet with him.

We saw (on day 18), how the Lord revealed through Haggai that he would fill his new 'house' with 'greater glory' than the temple built by Solomon. After informing us that the Word 'made his dwelling among us', John writes that 'we have seen his glory, the glory of the one and only Son, who came from the Father, full of grace and truth' (John 1:14). He shows us that the glory of this new 'dwelling' is far greater than that of Solomon's 'house'. As the angelic army declared to the shepherds, the greatest or highest possible glory to God has now come to pass (Luke 2:14). Jesus Christ 'came from the Father' and 'has made him known' in all of his fullness. Incredibly, to all who receive him, who believe in his name, 'he gave the right to become children of God' (John 1:12). As Scripture says elsewhere: 'in Christ all the fullness of the Deity lives in bodily form, and in Christ you have been brought to fullness' (Colossians 2:9–10). In the words of Athanasius, Patriarch of Alexandra in the fourth century, 'only the Image of the Father could re-create the likeness of the Image of men.'[13] Through the presence of God among humankind – and now through the gathering of his people among the nations[14] – his salvation will 'reach to the ends of the earth' (Isaiah 49:6).

---

13 Athanasius, *St. Athanasius on the Incarnation: The Treatise De Incarnatione Verbi Dei*, trans. *The Religious of C. S. M. V.*, 2nd ed. (London: A. R. Mowbray, 1953), p.48.

14 As Oliver O'Donovan writes: 'The gathering of the congregation is the moment at which the people's identity is disclosed ... Hence the importance of "gathering" ... The [Christian] community is a political community by virtue of being a worshipping community' (*The Desire of the Nations: Rediscovering the roots of political theology* (Cambridge: Cambridge University

Yet we also saw (on day 18) that 'glory' does not just convey a sense of weightiness, importance or splendour. It suggests a vindication and salvation that contrasts with dishonour and suffering. This, in turn, is tinged with a hint of judgement. In this we are reminded of scriptures such as those describing the time when the people of Israel 'tested and rebelled against the Most High God and did not keep his testimonies' (Psalm 78:56 ESV):

He forsook *his dwelling* at Shiloh,
   the tent where he dwelt among mankind,
and delivered his power to captivity,
   his glory to the hand of the foe.
He gave his people over to the sword
   and vented his wrath on his heritage.
(Psalm 78:60–2)

This, of course, is also the implication of John's words when he observes that 'though the world was made through him, the world did not recognise him. He came to that which was his own, but his own did not receive him' (John 1:10–11).

So Christmas presents us all with a choice. Recognise Jesus as the one and only Son of God the Father. Or else remain in the darkness and reject him in whom is life and true enlightenment. If we receive him as the one who is full of grace and truth, then we become children born of God. As members of God's people, Christ himself dwells in us (Romans 8:9–11). We ourselves are God's temple – his dwelling-place (1 Corinthians 3:16). Through his people, Christ continues to be made known to every generation.

Press, 1996), p. 47). Graham Ward adds to this: 'The bodies of Christian believers, individual and collected, constitute and contest social and political meaning, institutional and behavioral norms, with respect to their dwelling in Christ and Christ in them' (Graham Ward, *The Politics of Discipleship: Becoming postmaterial citizens* (London: SCM Press, 2009), p. 188). Ward also notes that Blumenfeld 'recognizes "the critical, foundational role that the body of Jesus plays," … The *ekklesia* is, for Blumenfeld, the heart of the new political community (the *polis*) that Paul is committed to forging' (Ward, *Politics of Discipleship*, p. 245, commenting on Bruno Blumenfeld, *The Political Paul: Democracy and kingship in Paul's thought* (London: Bloomsbury, 2003), p. 215).

Day 20

We bring life to 'those who are being saved' and death to 'those who are perishing' (2 Corinthians 2:15–16).

We can now understand why John so intricately brought together in his introduction the ideas of the Baptiser's testimony and God dwelling among us. It is not just that we continue to testify to what Jesus has done. Remarkably, collectively, together, as the 'assembly' of believers – that is, the 'Church' – we are now the body of Christ (Ephesians 5:23, 29–30; Colossians 1:18, 24).

The apostle Paul wrote that this is 'the mystery that has been kept hidden for ages and generations, but is now disclosed to the Lord's people' (Colossians 1:26). Namely, 'Christ in you, the hope of glory' (Colossians 1:27). Jesus said that 'the reason I was born and came into the world is to testify to the truth' (John 18:37). Now it is us – the family of believers, regularly gathering together as the assembly of God's children – who serve as 'a witness to testify concerning that light' so that through us 'all might believe' (John 1:7). Now it is through the Church that God makes known Christ's afflictions (Colossians 1:24). Now it is we who continue to bear witness to the resurrected Jesus and make known the hope of glory (Colossians 1:27).

This is 'the incarnational reality' of what it means to be a follower of Christ – and to live human life to the full. For, 'if we are children, then we are heirs – heirs of God and co-heirs with Christ, if indeed we share in his sufferings in order that we may also share in his glory' (Romans 8:17).

Pause to ponder

- In what ways are other believers integral to your life and witness?
- How does the appearance of Christ as 'the image of the invisible God' (Colossians 1:15) affect your understanding of what it means for you to have been created 'in the image of God' (Genesis 1:27)?

Day 21
Another Christmas night

For God so loved the world that he gave his one and only Son, that whoever believes in him shall not perish but have eternal life. For God did not send his Son into the world to condemn the world, but to save the world through him. Whoever believes in him is not condemned, but whoever does not believe stands condemned already because they have not believed in the name of God's one and only Son. This is the verdict: light has come into the world, but people loved darkness instead of light because their deeds were evil. Everyone who does evil hates the light, and will not come into the light for fear that their deeds will be exposed. But whoever lives by the truth comes into the light, so that it may be seen plainly that what they have done has been done in the sight of God. (John 3:16–21)

Quick glance

Early in Christ's ministry, under the cover of night, a member of the Jewish ruling council approaches Jesus. This teacher of Israel, Nicodemus, privately acknowledges that Jesus 'has come from God'. Jesus stresses that he came as the promised Saviour of the world to preserve life for God's people. He goes on to describe himself as the light that 'has come into the world'. He also opens up a fresh perspective on the metaphor for Nicodemus: 'whoever lives by the truth comes into the light'. By implication, those who do *not* live by the truth instead seek to *avoid* the light. This, Jesus says, is because they 'fear that their deeds will be exposed'. Whoever does not believe in Jesus, living by the truth of his light, 'stands condemned already'. Jesus seems implicitly to rebuke Nicodemus. It is but a gentle rebuke, though, with an explicit invitation for the member of the Jewish ruling council – and us – to come 'into the light'. John suggests in later chapters that by the time of Jesus' death, Nicodemus, like Joseph of Arimathea, may have been a secret believer.

In-depth reflection

Picture the scene: it was early in Christ's ministry, 'in Jerusalem at the Passover Festival' (John 2:23). At that time, the Jews were demanding that Jesus prove his authority to them (John 2:18). Under the cover of night, a member of the Jewish ruling council approaches Jesus. This teacher of Israel, Nicodemus, privately acknowledges that Jesus 'has come from God. For no one could perform the signs you are doing if God were not with him' (John 3:2).

They then engage in an exchange that consists of two parts. In the first, Jesus addresses the need for everyone to be 'born of the Spirit' if they are to 'enter the kingdom of God' (John 3:5–8). In the second, he begins by explaining that he 'came from heaven' and 'must be lifted up, that everyone who believes may have eternal life in him' (John 3:11–15). These two lessons are reminiscent of the groundwork that we saw (on day 4) laid in Exodus. There, remember, we saw that Jesus would 'come down from heaven ... that everyone who looks on the Son and believes in him should have eternal life' (John 6:38–40 ESV).

Jesus continues his lesson by stressing two conclusions for the teacher Nicodemus. The first is one of the most famous verses in the Gospels: 'For God so loved the world that he gave his one and only Son, that whoever believes in him shall not perish but have eternal life.' The second is like it: 'For God did not send his Son into the world to condemn the world, but to save the world through him' (John 3:16, 17). Both explain the purpose why 'the Word became flesh and made his dwelling among us' (John 1:14). He came as the promised Saviour of the world to preserve life for God's people.

Another Christmas night

Jesus went on to describe himself as the light that 'has come into the world' (John 3:19). This is the same imagery with which John introduced his Gospel: 'In him was life, and that life was the light of all mankind. The light shines in the darkness, and the darkness has not overcome it' (John 1:4–5). Later, Jesus would tell the people: 'I am the light of the world. Whoever follows me will never walk in darkness, but will have the light of life' (John 8:12).

We have already noted use of this light and darkness metaphor (most notably on days 9–10) in connection with the promised Messiah. From Isaiah, we learned how God would establish his kingdom of justice and righteousness for ever over the peoples of all the nations. Now that this 'light has come into the world', we can rejoice with Isaiah that God has 'enlarged the nation' of his people and has 'increased their joy' (Isaiah 9:3).

Yet Jesus also opens up a fresh perspective on the metaphor for Nicodemus. Yes, light has at last come into the world and 'whoever lives by the truth comes into the light'. By implication, however, not everybody lives by the truth. Jesus 'came from the Father, full of grace and truth' (John 1:14). So it should not be a surprise, Jesus tells the 'teacher of Israel', that those who do *not* live by the truth instead seek to *avoid* the light.

Despite the prospect of facing life beyond death in the same endless darkness and 'shadow of death' as they presently live, 'people [love] darkness instead of light'. Those who rebel against God and despise his good plans for us are repelled by the fullness of his grace and truth, as revealed in Christ. It is, Jesus says, because they 'fear that their deeds will be exposed' that they 'will not come into the light' (John 3:19–20). Whoever does not believe in Jesus, living by the truth of his light, 'stands condemned already' (v. 18).

As a scholar, Nicodemus would have been well aware of the comfort to be found in the lament of Psalm 23 (ESV): 'Even though I walk through the valley of the *shadow of death*, I will fear no evil, for you are with me'. He would, however, also have been familiar with the challenge associated with the same word (translated 'utter darkness') in Psalm 107, in which 'the redeemed of the LORD' (v. 2) tell their story:

> Some sat in darkness, in *utter darkness*,
>   prisoners suffering in iron chains,
> because they rebelled against God's commands
>   and despised the plans of the Most High.
> So he subjected them to bitter labour;
>   they stumbled, and there was no one to help.
> Then they cried to the LORD in their trouble,
>   and he saved them from their distress.
> He brought them out of darkness, the *utter darkness*,
>   and broke away their chains.
> Let them give thanks to the LORD for his unfailing love
>   and his wonderful deeds for mankind,
> for he breaks down gates of bronze
>   and cuts through bars of iron.
> (Psalm 107:10–16)

Jesus seems implicitly to rebuke Nicodemus. For, at the start of their exchange, remember, we were told: 'He came to Jesus at night' (John 3:2). It is but a gentle rebuke, though, with an explicit invitation for the member of the Jewish ruling council – and us – to come 'into the light'.

We are not immediately told how Nicodemus responded. Later, though, we are presented with a couple of clues. The people of Jerusalem began to ask about Jesus, 'Have the authorities really concluded that he is the Messiah?' and 'When the Messiah comes, will he perform more signs than this man?' (John 7:26, 31). When 'the Pharisees heard the crowd whispering such things ... the chief priests and the Pharisees sent temple guards to arrest him' (John 7:32). They were unsuccessful in their mission, however, and returned empty-handed. When asked to explain their failure, they replied: 'No one ever spoke the way this man does' (John 7:46). This prompted angry disbelief from the Pharisees. Nicodemus, however, spoke up in their defence, asking: 'Does our law condemn a man without first hearing him to find out what he has been doing?' (John 7:51).

The second clue comes after Jesus' crucifixion. Joseph of Arimathea 'was a disciple of Jesus, but secretly because he feared

Another Christmas night

the Jewish leaders' (John 19:38). 'With Pilate's permission,' we are told, 'he came and took the body away.' Crucially, the record adds: 'He was accompanied by Nicodemus, the man who earlier had visited Jesus at night' (John 19:39). In accordance with Jewish burial customs, the two of them wrapped Jesus' body with a mixture of about 75 pounds (35 kg) of myrrh and aloes that Nicodemus had brought along. They then laid Jesus in a tomb in a garden in the place where Jesus was crucified (John 19:40–2). John explains when this took place: 'Now it was the day of Preparation, and the next day was to be a special Sabbath' (John 19:31). Interestingly, Luke is even more explicit about the timing:

> It was Preparation Day, and the Sabbath was about to begin. The women who had come with Jesus from Galilee followed Joseph and saw the tomb and how his body was laid in it. Then they went home and … rested on the Sabbath in obedience to the commandment.
> (Luke 23:54–6)

For John, it is enough to point out the contrast that Nicodemus was 'the man who earlier had visited Jesus at night'. By the time of Jesus' death, like Joseph of Arimathea, Nicodemus may have been a secret believer. This time he was coming while it was still day. Night was coming, but the light had not been overcome by it. The testimony of Nicodemus invites us to sing the carol:

> On Christmas night all Christians sing
> to hear the news the angels bring:
> news of great joy, news of great mirth,
> news of our merciful King's birth.
>
> Then why should men on earth be sad,
> since our Redeemer made us glad,
> when from our sin He set us free,
> all for to gain our liberty?

Day 21

When sin departs before His grace,
then life and health come in its place,
angels and men with joy may sing,
all for to see the newborn King.

All out of darkness we have light,
which made the angels sing this night:
'Glory to God and peace to men,
now and forevermore. Amen.'[1]

Pause to ponder
- What things in your life do you try to hide from God's kingdom of light?
- In what ways could you be more open with others in talking about the kingdom of God and questions of eternity?

---

1 Luke Wadding (*c.* 1628–91), 'On Christmas Night All Christians Sing', Hymnary.org: https://hymnary.org/text/on_christmas_night_all_christians_sing (accessed 1 December 2023).

Day 22
Free at last

When the set time had fully come, God sent his Son, born of a woman, born under the law, to redeem those under the law, that we might receive adoption to sonship. Because you are his sons, God sent the Spirit of his Son into our hearts, the Spirit who calls out, '*Abba*, Father.' So you are no longer a slave, but God's child; and since you are his child, God has made you also an heir.
(Galatians 4:4–7)

Quick glance

This verse is striking for its double assertion that Christ was 'born'. In the New Testament, far more passages talk about the fact that Jesus was raised from death than that he was born. Yet, arguably, his incarnation is a far greater miracle than his resurrection. Although 'born of a woman', he was nevertheless able to preserve his own righteousness. The good news is not simply that Jesus was born. It is that he was born 'to redeem those under the law'. Through the birth of Jesus, God identified with us in our plight and thereby took repossession of us. As a result of his birth, those who turn to him are now able to obtain the everlasting life that was promised through the Law and the Prophets. Incredibly, even more than this, this happened 'that we might receive adoption to sonship'. As long promised, God himself has purchased our freedom. We are no longer slaves to sin, guilt or fear. Instead, we are now God's children: 'heirs having the hope of eternal life' and 'of the righteousness that is in keeping with faith'.

In-depth reflection

It seems that the closer we approach Christmas and the further we journey through the biblical story of Christ's birth, the less comfortable it risks becoming. Admittedly, it began with the insight that we are all cursed to die, separated from our Maker by our own folly. For most of Advent, however, we have been able to rediscover the excitement of one promise after another: a deliverer who will preserve life for ever; an Anointed King who will establish justice and righteousness for ever; a Separated One through whom all nations on earth will be blessed; a Redeemer who will free us from all guilt and blame.

Yet, in the last four days, we have heard notes of judgement in the praise of Bethlehem's angelic army; we have seen a foreshadowing of the crucifixion in the prophecies spoken over Jesus in the Temple; we have learned that the Church, as the present dwelling-place of God, should expect to make known Christ's afflictions; and we have heard Jesus himself warn that whoever does not believe in the name of God's one and only Son stands condemned.

Today we begin, then, by reaffirming the good news of Christmas: 'God sent his Son, born of a woman, born under the law, to redeem those under the law, that we might receive adoption to sonship.' This verse is striking for its double assertion that Christ was 'born'. It is even more remarkable because, after the four Gospel accounts, there are curiously few references to the birth of Jesus in the New Testament. Far more passages talk about the fact that he was raised from death than that he was born. Yet, arguably, his incarnation is a far greater miracle than his resurrection. After all, surely it should not be surprising that death could have no claim over the Author – that is, the 'Prince', 'Pioneer', 'Source' or 'Cause' – of all life? (Acts 3:15)[1] As Peter explained at Pentecost: 'It was impossible for death to keep its hold on him' (Acts 2:24). In contrast, it should continue to be mind-boggling that the infinite, eternally existent Creator of time and space chose

---

1 'The title points to royal prerogatives and princely power in the service of God.' George Johnston, 'Christ as Archegos: Short Studies', *New Testament Studies*, vol. 27, no. 3 (1981), p.381–5.

to be confined and contained within the finite 'tent' of a human body bound by space and time! It is truly amazing that the child foreseen by Isaiah (9:6) should be identified as the 'Everlasting Father' or, more literally, 'Father of eternity'.

Job observed that those 'born of woman … are of few days and full of trouble. They spring up like flowers and wither away; like fleeting shadows, they do not endure' (Job 14:1–2). Yet God sent his eternal Son to be 'born of a woman'. Bildad the Shuhite later rhetorically asked Job, 'How then can a mortal be righteous before God? How can one born of woman be pure?' (Job 25:4). The expected answer is, 'With man this is impossible.' Yet 'with God all things are possible' (Matthew 19:26). For humankind was originally created in God's image, righteous and pure. As we saw (on day 1), before the earth became 'corrupt in God's sight' (Genesis 6:11), everything that God made was 'very good' (Genesis 1:31). So, when God sent his Son, although 'born of a woman', he was nevertheless able to preserve his own righteousness and purity.

Yet God also sent his perfect Son to be 'born under the law'. Born as a member of God's chosen people, the descendants of Israel, Jesus was subject to the Law of Moses. He was born as a slave to God's law. Unlike every one of us, however, 'he committed no sin, and no deceit was found in his mouth' (1 Peter 2:22). Thus, 'now apart from the law the righteousness of God has been made known, to which the Law and the Prophets testify' (Romans 3:21). So 'God made him who had no sin to be sin for us, so that in him we might become the righteousness of God' (2 Corinthians 5:21).

This, then, is the miracle of miracles, the true 'magic' of Christmas: 'God sent his Son, born of a woman, born under the law, to redeem those under the law, that we might receive adoption to sonship.' No wonder the whole of human history is rightly understood in relation to his birth! 'The year of the Lord' (Anno Domini or AD) and 'Before Christ' (BC) were defined by his birth, not his resurrection. 'All history either points towards or flows from that moment when the Word became flesh and all space is ordered to and guided by

Day 22

that *locus* where the Creator and the creature are united in the Divine Person of the Word.'[2]

The good news, of course, is not simply that Jesus was born. It is that he was born 'to redeem those under the law'. Under the Law of Moses, anyone who was forced to sell themselves into slavery could be redeemed. That is, any relative could buy back their freedom. Alternatively, if they themselves prospered, they could buy back their own freedom (Leviticus 25:49).

We have seen (particularly on days 11, 13 and 19) that our promised redemption is from sin and death. As the psalmist wrote:

> If you, LORD, kept a record of sins,
> Lord, who could stand?
> But with you there is forgiveness,
> so that we can, with reverence, serve you ...
>
> Israel, put your hope in the LORD,
> for with the LORD is unfailing love
> and with him is full redemption.
> He himself will redeem Israel
> from all their sins.
> (Psalm 130:3–4, 7–8)

Through the prophet Hosea, the Lord also declared: 'I will deliver this people from the power of the grave; I will redeem them from death' (Hosea 13:14). So, through the birth of Jesus, God identified with us in our plight and thereby took repossession of us. As a result of his birth, those who turn to him have been freed from sin and death. As a consequence of his birth, we are now able to obtain the everlasting life that was promised through the Law and the Prophets.

Yet, incredibly, there is even more to this good news. Yes, Jesus was born. Yes, he was born 'to redeem those under the law'. More

---

[2] Fr Maximilian, 'Christ the Centerpiece of All Creation', The Absolute Primacy of Christ, 29 October 2018: https://absoluteprimacyofchrist.org/christ-the-centerpiece-of-all-creation (accessed 7 December 2023).

than this, though, this happened 'that we might receive adoption to sonship'. As Jesus himself taught:

> Very truly I tell you, everyone who sins is a slave to sin. Now a slave has no permanent place in the family, but a son belongs to it for ever. So if the Son sets you free, you will be free indeed.
> (John 8:34–6)

As long promised, God himself has purchased our freedom. We are no longer slaves to sin; no longer slaves to guilt; no longer slaves to fear. Instead, we are now God's children. This means, as the apostle Paul wrote to the Galatians, 'God has made you also an heir' (Galatians 4:7): 'heirs having the hope of eternal life' (Titus 3:7); heirs 'of the righteousness that is in keeping with faith' (Hebrews 11:7); and heirs 'of the gracious gift of life' (1 Peter 3:7). As Peter also declared, in the early days of the Church:

> Indeed, beginning with Samuel, all the prophets who have spoken have foretold these days. And you are heirs of the prophets and of the covenant God made with your fathers. He said to Abraham, 'Through your offspring all peoples on earth will be blessed.' When God raised up his servant, he sent him first to you to bless you by turning each of you from your wicked ways.
> (Acts 3:24–6)

Having received eternal life, freedom from slavery to sin, and union in Christ as heirs to all that is his, our right response should be one of comfort and joy. The concluding words of the civil rights activist Revd Martin Luther King Jr's 'I have a dream' speech, delivered in Washington, DC, on 28 August 1963, could have originally been conceived as a celebration of Christmas: 'In the words of the old Negro spiritual: "Free at last! Free at last! Thank God Almighty, we are free at last!"'[3] As the carol 'God Rest Ye Merry, Gentlemen' puts it:

---

3 '"I Have a Dream" Speech', History.com, 30 November 2017: https://www.history.com/topics/black-history/i-have-a-dream-speech (accessed 1 December 2023).

Day 22

'Fear not,' then said the angel,
'Let nothing you affright;
this day is born a Savior
of a pure virgin bright,
to free all those who trust in Him
from Satan's pow'r and might.'

O tidings of comfort and joy,
comfort and joy;
O tidings of comfort and joy.[4]

Pause to ponder
- What implications of being God's child and heir might you seek to make a greater reality in your daily life?
- Are there areas of your life in which the freedom of Christ has yet to liberate you fully – from sin, guilt or fear – even fear of death?

---

[4] From the anonymous eighteenth-century English carol 'God Rest Ye Merry, Gentlemen', Hymnary.org: https://hymnary.org/text/god_rest_ye_merry_gentlemen (accessed 1 December 2023).

Day 23
Interchange in Christ

Have this mind among yourselves, which is yours in Christ Jesus, who, though he was in the form of God, did not count equality with God a thing to be grasped, but made himself nothing, taking the form of a servant, being born in the likeness of men. And being found in human form, he humbled himself by becoming obedient to the point of death, even death on a cross.
(Philippians 2:5–8 ESV)

Quick glance

Christ's nativity, we have asserted, is the greatest moment in the history of the universe. Yet the purpose of his birth and the means by which he redeemed 'those under the law' was his death. The problem, remember, was our rejection of God and his perfect ways. Although we were made in God's likeness, we strove to become masters of our own fate. Instead, we became slaves to corruption and death. In contrast, Jesus set aside equality with God and shared in our humanity in order that, by his death, we might have life and be freed from our fear of death. This is not so much a reversal as an epic exchange – or interchange – in Christ. Christ identified himself with us, sharing in our humanity, in order that whoever identifies themselves with him might share in his righteousness, resurrection life, and relationship with God the Father. There is an 'incarnational reality' to our interchange in Christ, however, that demands we share in his experience of reversal. Being united 'with Christ' and 'in Christ' means sharing in his sufferings, so that we may also share in his glory.

In-depth reflection

I wonder whether you noticed that we skipped over one key part of the story yesterday. We omitted to observe the *means* by which Jesus purchased our freedom. In their letter to the believers in Philippi, Paul and Timothy address this crucial point. 'Being born in the likeness of men', Christ Jesus became 'obedient to the point of death, even death on a cross' (Philippians 2:7–8 ESV).

Christ's nativity, we have asserted, is the greatest moment in the history of the universe. Yet the purpose of Jesus' birth, and the means by which he redeemed 'those under the law' (Galatians 4:5), was his death. As we look on his manger, we can already glimpse the looming shadow of his cross. Evidently, this had to be so. The best explanation for this is perhaps to be found in the book of Hebrews:

> Since the children have flesh and blood, he too shared in their humanity so that by his death he might break the power of him who holds the power of death – that is, the devil – and free those who all their lives were held in slavery by their fear of death. For surely it is not angels he helps, but Abraham's descendants. For this reason he had to be made like them, fully human in every way, in order that he might become a merciful and faithful high priest in service to God, and that he might make atonement for the sins of the people.
> (Hebrews 2:14–17)

The problem, remember, was our rejection of God and his perfect ways. We were made in his likeness but sought to do things our own way. As though we could improve on his perfect design, we strove to become masters of our own fate. Instead, we became slaves to corruption and death. In contrast, Jesus – who was 'in very nature God' – 'made himself nothing by taking the very nature of a servant'. Setting aside equality with God and 'being made in human likeness', he took on flesh and blood to share in our humanity. 'Being found in appearance as a man', our Redeemer chose to become 'fully human in every way'.

Interchange in Christ

Nothing could be more dramatic than this cosmic reversal. It is a theme that we saw introduced by Hannah (on day 8). Remember: she foresaw, for example, that 'the LORD brings death and makes alive; he brings down to the grave and raises up. The LORD sends poverty and wealth; he humbles and he exalts' (1 Samuel 2:6–7). What Christ has done, however, is of a different order. It is not just that his status was reversed. It is not simply that he was 'in very nature God' and 'made himself nothing'. For, his reversed status is the very means by which our fate is finally reversed:

> Once you were alienated from God and were enemies in your minds because of your evil behaviour. But now he has reconciled you by Christ's physical body through death to present you holy in his sight, without blemish and free from accusation … (Colossians 1:21–2)

Christ shared in our humanity in order that, by his death, we might have life and be freed from our fear of death. The Lord brought his Son down to the grave in order to raise us up alive. The Lord sent his Son into poverty in order that we might share in his eternal wealth. The Lord humbled himself so that he might exalt us who, in our pride, had turned our backs on him. As Paul and Timothy wrote to the church in Corinth: 'For you know the grace of our Lord Jesus Christ, that though he was rich, yet for your sake he became poor, so that you through his poverty might become rich' (2 Corinthians 8:9). And again, as we previously observed (on day 22): 'God made him who had no sin to be sin for us, so that in him we might become the righteousness of God' (2 Corinthians 5:21).

This is not so much a reversal as an epic exchange – or interchange – in Christ. 'Great indeed, we confess, is the mystery of godliness: He was manifested in the flesh' (1 Timothy 3:16 ESV). As the Russian Orthodox St John of Kronstadt taught:

> The Word became flesh! … in order to make us earthly beings into heavenly ones, in order to make sinners into saints; in order to raise us up from corruption into incorruption, from

Day 23

earth to heaven; from enslavement to sin and the devil – into the glorious freedom of children of God; from death – into immortality, in order to make us sons of God and to seat us together with Him upon the Throne as His royal children.'[1]

As we observed (on days 16 and 22), but now read in the words of another writer, Jesus 'took on our flesh so as to bring life to that which had been touched by death, and he took on our human nature so as to bring freedom to that which had been enslaved by sin'. God came 'to enter into complete union with his people and, by virtue of that union, undo the result of sin entering the world'.[2]

As a consequence of what took place in Bethlehem around two millennia ago, we are no longer destined to remain for ever separated from our creator. Instead, Jesus declares: 'The one who believes in me will live, even though they die' (John 11:25). For 'whoever wants to save their life will lose it, but whoever loses their life for me will find it' (Matthew 16:25). This is the fulfilment of the divine promises made repeatedly since before the beginning of recorded human history. This is the glory that the angels declared when God 'made his dwelling among us' in human likeness:

> This grace was given us in Christ Jesus before the beginning of time, but it has now been revealed through the appearing of our Saviour, Christ Jesus, who has destroyed death and has brought life and immortality to light through the gospel.
> (2 Timothy 1:9–10)

As the second-century Greek theologian Irenaeus put it: 'Christ became what we are, in order that we might become what he is.'[3]

---

[1] 'The Word Became Flesh: A sermon by St John of Kronstadt on the nativity of Christ', St Nicholas Russian Orthodox Church (McKinney, TX), Orthodox.net (no date): https://www.orthodox.net/nativity/nativity-sjok-2.html (accessed 28 March 2022).

[2] Mike May, 'The Incarnation of Jesus Christ: The key to our redemption', The Catholic Voice, 7 January 2021: https://catholicvoiceomaha.com/the-incarnation-of-jesus-christ-the-key-to-our-redemption (accessed 28 March 2022).

[3] Morna Hooker, *From Adam to Christ: Essays on Paul*, 2nd edn (Eugene, OR: Wipf & Stock, 2008), p. 26.

Interchange in Christ

Christ identified himself with us, sharing in our humanity, in order that whoever identifies themselves with him might share in his righteousness, resurrection life and relationship with God the Father:

> So will it be with the resurrection of the dead. The body that is sown is perishable, it is raised imperishable; it is sown in dishonour, it is raised in glory; it is sown in weakness, it is raised in power; it is sown a natural body, it is raised a spiritual body. (1 Corinthians 15:42–4)

Of course, all this has huge ramifications. As we saw (on day 20), being united 'with Christ' and 'in Christ' means sharing in his sufferings, so that we may also share in his glory (Romans 8:17; 1 Peter 4:13). As Paul recognised, there is an 'incarnational reality' to our interchange in Christ that demands we share in his experience of reversal: 'I want to know Christ – yes, to know the power of his resurrection and participation in his sufferings, becoming like him in his death, and so, somehow, attaining to the resurrection from the dead' (Philippians 3:10–11).

We who recognise that the appearing of Christ 'has brought life and immortality to light' are called to 'have the same mindset as Christ Jesus'. We are summoned to be those who 'in humility value others above yourselves, not looking to your own interests but each of you to the interests of the others' (Philippians 2:3–4). We are supposed to be those who 'join together in following [the] example' of Paul and Timothy (Philippians 3:17) by showing 'genuine concern for [the] welfare' of others (Philippians 2:20) and taking a public stand against injustice, as Paul and Silas did in Philippi (Acts 16:35–9).

Jesus freed 'those who all their lives were held in slavery by their fear of death' (Hebrews 2:15). So the apostle Paul tells each of us in Christ: 'Obey from your heart the pattern of teaching that has now claimed your allegiance. You have been set free from sin and have become slaves to righteousness' (Romans 6:17–18). Jesus became 'obedient to death'. So, too, we are called 'to be obedient to Jesus

Day 23

Christ' (1 Peter 1:2), to 'participate in his sufferings' and to 'fill up' in our flesh 'what is still lacking in regard to Christ's afflictions, for the sake of his body, which is the church' (Colossians 1:24). 'For it has been granted to [us] on behalf of Christ not only to believe in him, but also to suffer for him' (Philippians 1:29).

Pause to ponder

- Do you tend to think of Jesus more as the 'Son of Man', 'fully human in every way' (Hebrews 2:17) – or as the 'Son of God', in whom 'all the fullness of the Deity lives in bodily form' (Colossians 2:9)? What might a deeper appreciation of the other title mean for you this Advent season?
- What do you think it might mean for you to participate 'in Christ's sufferings' and to become 'like him in his death' as you seek more fully the interests of those still 'held in slavery by their fear of death'?

Day 24
The great red dragon

A great sign appeared in heaven: a woman clothed with the sun, with the moon under her feet and a crown of twelve stars on her head. She was pregnant and cried out in pain as she was about to give birth. Then another sign appeared in heaven: an enormous red dragon with seven heads and ten horns and seven crowns on its heads. Its tail swept a third of the stars out of the sky and flung them to the earth. The dragon stood in front of the woman who was about to give birth, so that it might devour her child the moment he was born. She gave birth to a son, a male child, who 'will rule all the nations with an iron sceptre.' And her child was snatched up to God and to his throne. The woman fled into the wilderness to a place prepared for her by God, where she might be taken care of for 1,260 days.
(Revelation 12:1–6)

Quick glance

Like the science fiction and fantasy of our own generation, John's second account of Jesus' birth, in Revelation 12, addresses timeless concerns such as the inner conflict between good and evil. Drawing on images elsewhere in Scripture, John uses the woman to represent the people of God. He depicts God's chosen people giving 'birth to a son, a male child, who "will rule all the nations with an iron sceptre"' – the one foretold by Balaam and by Jacob. The great dragon, John tells us, is none other than 'that ancient serpent called the devil, or Satan, who leads the whole world astray'. He depicts the cosmic conflict that has been raging since the dawn

Day 24

of humankind and shows us the decisive outcome of this spiritual warfare. The dragon sought to devour the Messiah the moment he was born. At Christ's birth, however, our deliverance was sealed. So the dragon returns to persecuting God's people. Like the people of Israel during their wilderness experience, we can expect both persecution and protection. Yet, because of Christmas Day, as we await Christ's return, we have assurance that we have already triumphed in Christ.

In-depth reflection

Every nativity scene should have a seven-headed red dragon lurking ominously, ready to devour the infant King. As well as being attention grabbing, it would arguably be more biblical! Three of the Gospel writers record an account of Jesus' birth that serves their purposes. Matthew's features God-seeking magi from the east as part of his emphasis that, in fulfilment of Old Testament Scripture, God's message of new life is for the Gentile nations as well as for the descendants of Israel. Mark's account skips over the nativity to focus on his challenge for each individual to be baptised in response to the empty tomb. Luke's evidence-based approach documents the first eyewitnesses, namely the shepherds. John has two stabs at the 'magic' of Christmas. His first, in John 1, grapples philosophically with the mystery of how the eternal Creator planned from before the creation of time and space to enter his own creation. His second, in Revelation 12, adopts the imagery of apocalyptic literature, a genre with which most Westerners are strangely unfamiliar.

I say 'strangely' because many of the same features can be found in the science fiction and fantasy of our own generation. Just like many recent books and films, for example J. R. R. Tolkien's *The Lord of the Rings*, Stanley Kubrick's *2001: A Space Odyssey* and the Wachowskis' *Matrix* franchise, the author's message and intent are typically time-collapsed, clothed in symbolism and communicated by otherworldly characters with superpowers. Whether making use of traditional fictional forms of magic, or barely imaginable technology, these profound stories resonate with readers and viewers. Crucially, although they often appear to tell of the distant past or distant future, in reality they address the timeless concerns of their contemporary audiences, such as the inner conflict between good and evil.

So, if our nativity scenes include Matthew's magi and Luke's shepherds, why not also John's dragon?

Subconsciously, perhaps we resist this idea because we are uncomfortable with its reminder of our daily and lifelong unsuccessful struggle with sin and death. Yet it should not make us uncomfortable. Rather, it should encourage us greatly. For it also reminds us that God sent 'his own Son in the likeness of sinful flesh to be a sin offering' (Romans 8:3). It reminds us that 'Christ redeemed us from the curse of the law by becoming a curse for us … so that in Christ Jesus the blessing of Abraham might come to the Gentiles, so that we might receive the promised Spirit through faith' (Galatians 3:13–14 ESV).

The key to understanding apocalyptic writing in the Bible is recognising that Scripture draws on its own pool of images. We do not need to seek additional historical or cultural references that may since have been lost to us. John's nativity begins with a woman crowned in splendour. There are two places in Scripture where crowned women are portrayed. The first is in Ezekiel 23:42, where the two kingdoms of Judah and Israel are depicted as unfaithful women, crowned by their lovers. The second is in Esther 2:17, when King Xerxes, 'who ruled over 127 provinces stretching from India to Cush' (Esther 1:1), made a young woman from the tribe of Benjamin his queen and 'set a royal crown on her head'. In contrast with unfaithful Israel, Hadassah, also known as Esther, was faithful and 'won the favour of everyone who saw her' (Esther 2:15). Esther 9 records how she was able to exercise the full authority of the king and delivered the people of God from a plot to destroy them.

John's crowned woman, 'clothed with the sun, with the moon under her feet', appears also to draw on Joseph's dream, in which 'the sun and moon and eleven stars were bowing down to [him]'

(Genesis 37:9). His father and brothers recognised that this vision meant they would one day bow down to Joseph, as indeed later came to pass.

Later, John adds: 'The woman was given the two wings of a great eagle, so that she might fly to the place prepared for her in the wilderness' (Revelation 12:14). This brings to mind a description of the people of Israel when the Lord led them out of Egypt into the wilderness: 'You yourselves have seen what I did to Egypt, and how I carried you on eagles' wings and brought you to myself' (Exodus 19:4).

At the end of the chapter, John is explicit that the woman's offspring are 'those who keep God's commands and hold fast their testimony about Jesus' (Revelation 12:17). Taken together, it is clear that the woman represents the people of God, and the twelve stars signify the tribes of Israel.

John then adopts an image from the Prophets that described Israel as a pregnant woman trying to bring salvation to the earth. Isaiah is clear: by themselves, the people of God were unable to achieve this, but the Lord would cause their dead to live:

> As a pregnant woman about to give birth
>   writhes and cries out in her pain,
>   so were we in your presence, LORD.
> We were with child, we writhed in labour,
>   but we gave birth to wind.
> We have not brought salvation to the earth,
>   and the people of the world have not come to life.
>
> But your dead will live, LORD;
>   their bodies will rise ...
> (Isaiah 26:17–19)

Similarly, Micah connects Israel's hopes for a messianic King to the pains of a woman in labour. He too disillusions the people, explaining that their own efforts will only lead to exile, but that the Lord will redeem them:

> Why do you now cry aloud –
>   have you no king?
> Has your ruler perished,
>   that pain seizes you like that of a woman in labour?
> Writhe in agony, Daughter Zion,
>   like a woman in labour,
> for now you must leave the city
>   to camp in the open field.
> You will go to Babylon;
>   there you will be rescued.
> There the LORD will redeem you
>   out of the hand of your enemies.
> (Micah 4:9–10)

It is striking that the first mention of labour pains in the Bible comes as part of the curse following the Fall, when God tells Eve: 'I will make your pains in childbearing very severe; with painful labour you will give birth to children' (Genesis 3:16).

So it is that John depicts God's chosen people giving 'birth to a son, a male child, who "will rule all the nations with an iron sceptre"'. This, we should recognise (from day 5), is the one foretold by Balaam and by Jacob: the sceptre that would 'rise out of Israel' (Numbers 24:17); and the sceptre that would 'not depart from Judah … until he to whom it belongs shall come and the obedience of the nations shall be his' (Genesis 49:10). The context of the psalm quoted by John in verse 5 makes clear that the 'male child' is indeed 'the Lord's Anointed', the one installed by him as King and, moreover, his Son (Psalm 2).

About the identity of the dragon, John leaves us in no doubt. The great dragon, he tells us, is none other than 'that ancient serpent, who is called the devil and Satan, the deceiver of the whole world' (Revelation 12:9 ESV). Adopting the language of another apocalyptic Bible passage, John reminds us that, since the garden of Eden, this dragon has been intent on persecuting God's people: 'it reached the host of the heavens, and it threw some of the starry host down to the earth and trampled on them' (Daniel 8:10). Now,

Day 24

at the point where God's long-promised Messiah is about to be born, 'the dragon stood in front of the woman who was about to give birth, so that it might devour her child the moment he was born'.

This is truly the most momentous – and most 'magical' – point in the history of the universe. We saw at the start of Advent (on day 1) that an offspring promised to the first humans would crush the serpent's head but that, until that time, sin and death would prevail. Since the dawn of humankind, a cosmic conflict has thus been raging. Most of the time, we are blissfully unaware of this spiritual battle. Occasionally, however, we are given glimpses of this true state of affairs. For instance, the prophet Elisha saw a chariot and horses of fire when Elijah was taken up to heaven (2 Kings 2:11–12). Later, when surrounded by the king of Aram and his army, the Lord opened the eyes of Elisha's servant and he 'saw the hills full of horses and chariots of fire all round Elisha' (2 Kings 6:17). In another instance, while the prophet Daniel was praying, he had a vision of a man: 'His body was like topaz, his face like lightning, his eyes like flaming torches, his arms and legs like the gleam of burnished bronze, and his voice like the sound of a multitude' (Daniel 10:6). This heavenly man, reminiscent of the cherubim guarding the way to the tree of life in Genesis 3:24, and associated with the glory of the Lord in Ezekiel 10, explained to Daniel:

> Since the first day that you set your mind to gain understanding and to humble yourself before your God, your words were heard, and I have come in response to them. The prince of the Persian kingdom resisted me twenty-one days. Then Michael, one of the chief princes, came to help me, because I was detained there with the king of Persia.
> (Daniel 10:12–13)

Likewise, when Jesus was praying before his crucifixion, we are told that 'an angel from heaven appeared to him and strengthened him' (Luke 22:43). In one of his letters, the apostle Paul also notes: 'Our struggle is not against flesh and blood, but against

The great red dragon

the rulers, against the authorities, against the powers of this dark world and against the spiritual forces of evil in the heavenly realms' (Ephesians 6:12).

Here in Revelation we are shown the decisive outcome of this spiritual warfare: 'Michael and his angels fought against the dragon, and the dragon and his angels fought back. But he was not strong enough, and they lost their place in heaven' (Revelation 12:7–8). The dragon sought to devour the Messiah the moment he was born. As soon as his mother gave birth, however, 'her child was snatched up to God and to his throne' (v. 5). The dragon's plans were foiled.

Notice that as far as John is concerned, the crucifixion and resurrection of Jesus do not even merit a mention at this stage. Not that John in any way diminishes their place in achieving our salvation. After all, his vision begins with the assertion that Jesus 'freed us from our sins by his blood' (Revelation 1:5). His vision of God's throne-room also affirms of Christ that he was 'slain, and with [his] blood [he] purchased for God persons from every tribe and language and people and nation' (Revelation 5:9). Later in this chapter, too, John declares that our triumph over the Accuser is 'by the blood of the Lamb' (Revelation 12:11).

Nevertheless, victory was snatched from Satan long before he might have thought that he had at last triumphed over God's people. For it was at Christ's birth, not his death, that our deliverance was sealed – in flesh and blood, when God was 'found in appearance as a man' (Philippians 2:8).

Then, as the vision continued, 'the dragon was enraged at the woman and went off to wage war against the rest of her offspring – those who keep God's commands and hold fast their testimony about Jesus' (Revelation 12:17). So John shows that the dragon returns to persecuting God's people. Yet the Accuser failed to destroy God's chosen ones in the days of Pharoah, of Esther and of Herod. He is even less capable of destroying God's church today. For we now live between the ascension and the return of Christ. This symbolic period of '1,260 days' (or 'a time, times and half a time' as it is formulated in v. 14, and '42 months' elsewhere in Revelation) is described (in vv. 6 and 14) as a wilderness experience. Like the

Day 24

people of Israel in their wilderness experience, after the Lord freed them from Egypt but before they entered the promised land, we can expect both persecution and protection. That ancient serpent called the devil, or Satan, will continue trying to lead the whole world astray.

Yet, because of Christmas Day, whatever trials and temptations may yet lie in store for us as we await Christ's return, we have the assurance that we have already triumphed in Christ. In him, we have a certain hope, based on the blood of Christ, the word of our testimony as we bear witness to Jesus, and our not shrinking from death – even as 'he humbled himself by becoming obedient to death' (Philippians 2:8). These truths John declares in his heavenly Christmas carol (the singing of which, sadly, appears to have gone out of fashion after the nineteenth century):[1]

> Now have come the salvation and the power
>   and the kingdom of our God,
>   and the authority of his Messiah.
> For the accuser of our brothers and sisters,
>   who accuses them before our God day and night,
>   has been hurled down.
> They triumphed over him
>   by the blood of the Lamb
>   and by the word of their testimony;
> they did not love their lives so much
>   as to shrink from death.
> Therefore rejoice, you heavens
>   and you who dwell in them!
> But woe to the earth and the sea,
>   because the devil has gone down to you!
> He is filled with fury,
>   because he knows that his time is short.
> (Revelation 12:10–12)

---

[1] An example of a once-popular rendition of this passage from Revelation is the hymn by John Kent (1766–1843): 'Now Is Come, Is Come the Salvation', Hymnary.org: https://hymnary.org/text/now_is_come_is_come_the_salvation (accessed 11 April 2022).

Rejoice, therefore, because 'the reason the Son of God appeared was to destroy the devil's work' (1 John 3:8). Even in the face of bereavement or when our own lives draw to a close, we can magnify 'the firstborn of all creation' who is also 'the firstborn from the dead' (Colossians 1:15, 18 ESV). May each of us be numbered among 'those who keep God's commands and hold fast their testimony about Jesus' (Revelation 12:17).

Pause to ponder
- How do you feel about the idea of there being a dragon at the nativity?
- What difference could this certain hope – the assurance that we have already triumphed in Christ – make to you in the year ahead as we daily await his second advent?

Day 25
Christmas epilogue

'I, Jesus, have sent my angel to give you this testimony for the churches. I am the Root and the Offspring of David, and the bright Morning Star.'

The Spirit and the bride say, 'Come!' And let the one who hears say, 'Come!' Let the one who is thirsty come; and let the one who wishes take the free gift of the water of life.
(Revelation 22:16–17)

Summoned to curse God's people (on day 5), the prophet Balaam saw that a star or ruler would come out of Jacob. At the very end of the Bible, Jesus calls himself the 'bright Morning Star'. The bright morning star is, in fact, Venus – the last light in the sky when the light of all other stars disappears before the rising sun. So, as an image of the Messiah, it conveys how his appearance on earth was the last awaited sign before the end of darkness. As Isaiah foretold, 'The people walking in darkness have seen a great light' (Isaiah 9:2). Nothing else needs to happen before the promised Day of the Lord dawns. From an eternal perspective, just a brief few minutes remain between Jesus' life on earth and his return in judgement. We live not just in the last days; we live in the last minutes.

One time, when travelling from Judea to Galilee, Jesus and his disciples 'came to a town in Samaria called Sychar, near the plot of ground Jacob had given to his son Joseph':

Jacob's well was there, and Jesus, tired as he was from the journey, sat down by the well. It was about noon.

When a Samaritan woman came to draw water, Jesus said

Christmas epilogue

to her, 'Will you give me a drink?' (His disciples had gone into the town to buy food.)

The Samaritan woman said to him, 'You are a Jew and I am a Samaritan woman. How can you ask me for a drink?' (For Jews do not associate with Samaritans.)

Jesus answered her, 'If you knew the gift of God and who it is that asks you for a drink, you would have asked him and he would have given you living water.'
(John 4:5–10)

Jesus' Christmas present to each of us remains the same today as it was to the Samaritan woman on that day. So let whoever wishes 'take the free gift of the water of life'.

O holy night! The stars are brightly shining;
It is the night of the dear Savior's birth.
Long lay the world in sin and error pining,
Till He appeared and the soul felt its worth.
A thrill of hope – the weary world rejoices,
For yonder breaks a new and glorious morn!
Fall on your knees! O hear the angel voices!
O night divine, O night when Christ was born!
O night, O holy night, O night divine!

Truly He taught us to love one another;
His law is love and His gospel is peace.
Chains shall He break, for the slave is our brother,
And in His name all oppression shall cease.
Sweet hymns of joy in grateful chorus raise we;
Let all within us praise His holy name.
Christ is the Lord! O praise His name forever!
His pow'r and glory evermore proclaim!
His pow'r and glory evermore proclaim![1]

---

[1] From 'O Holy Night' (1847) by Placide Cappeau, tr. John Dwight, Hymnary.org: https://hymnary.org/text/o_holy_night_the_stars_are_brightly_shin (accessed 14 April 2022).

Acknowledgements

Here is a trustworthy saying that deserves full acceptance: Christ Jesus came into the world to save sinners – of whom I am the worst. But for that very reason I was shown mercy so that in me, the worst of sinners, Christ Jesus might display his immense patience as an example for those who would believe in him and receive eternal life. Now to the King eternal, immortal, invisible, the only God, be honour and glory for ever and ever. Amen.
(1 Timothy 1:15–17)

I have been privileged to have been consistently exposed to excellent Bible teaching as an adult. Many of my ideas will have been shaped by preachers that I have heard and authors whose Bible commentaries I have studied over the years. These are too many to recall or record without fear of boring the reader or of giving offence to any whom I might omit. Nevertheless, I should make particular mention, among many who made a memorable impression on me, of those whose ideas are noticeably reflected in this collection of devotions and whose studies are worth further investigation.

While living in Cambridge, I have benefited from contact with Bible scholars from around the world who have undertaken research at Tyndale House. Uppermost among these experts is my friend Peter Williams, its principal, with whom I have enjoyed many opportunities to delve deeply into Scripture and to share insights and discoveries – archaeological and astronomical, as well as biblical and theological ones.

The influence on my thinking of James Bejon, another Tyndale scholar, will be apparent to anyone familiar with his 2021 article

Acknowledgements

'The "Extraordinary Birth" Type-Scene'.[1] His social media posts are well worth following.

For cultural insights into the birth narratives and teachings of Jesus, the writings of Kenneth Bailey are essential reading. I shall always remember David and Margaret Hampshire with fondness for having introduced me to his books – namely *Poet & Peasant and Through Peasant's Eyes: A literary–cultural approach to the parables in Luke* (combined edition, Eerdmans, 1983) and *Jesus through Middle Eastern Eyes: Cultural studies in the Gospels* (SPCK, 2008).

It was a former Bible translator, Peter Kingston, who initiated studies of the Mamaindê (Northern Nambikwara) language in Brazil, who introduced me in 1993 to his insights into interchange in Christ, which I later found independently explored by Morna Hooker (see her 'Interchange in Christ', *Journal of Theological Studies*, vol. 22, no. 2 (1971), pp. 349–61).[2]

Table 5 and my thoughts on days 18 and 19 can be traced back to my reading, around the same period, of Stephen Farris's book *The Hymns of Luke's Infancy Narratives: Their origin, meaning and significance* (Continuum, 1985).

For a deeper appreciation of Malachi, I commend the writings of Anthony Petterson ('The Identity of "The Messenger of the Covenant" in Malachi 3:1 – Lexical and Rhetorical Analyses', *Bulletin for Biblical Research* 29 (2019); and *Haggai, Zechariah & Malachi*, Apollos Old Testament Commentary 25 (2012)) and Richard Blaylock ('My Messenger, the LORD, and the Messenger of the Covenant: Malachi 3:1 Revisited', *Southern Baptist Journal of Theology*, vol. 20, no. 3 (2016), pp. 69–95).

I am grateful to friends and others – especially my daughter, Emma, Tom Creedy at IVP and those who generously sent me feedback along with their commendations – whose conversations and suggestions helped to make this book more accessible and, I

---

[1] James Bejon, 'The "Extraordinary Birth" Type-Scene', Substack, 30 October 2021: https://jamesbejon.substack.com/p/the-extraordinary-birth-type-scene (accessed 1 December 2023).

[2] See also Neil Anderson, *Victory over the Darkness: Realizing the power of your identity in Christ* (Ventura, CA: Regal Books, 1990).

Day 25

trust, more enriching than it would otherwise have been. Credit for the 'twisted lyrics' anecdote of Day 12 belongs to a good friend and colleague, Susan Layman.

Lastly, this collection would not have come together at all if it had not been for my family: James and Emma, for whom my wife and I originally compiled the daily Advent verses; and my wife, Rebecca, who patiently permitted and encouraged me to produce this collection of devotions, even though she hoped after my last book that I would never write another!

Index of Scripture references

OLD TESTAMENT

Genesis
1:1–3 *51*
1:1–5 *58*
1:27 *136*
1:31 *5, 145*
2:7 *14*
3 *9*
3:7 *27*
3:14–15 *3*
3:14–23 *27*
3:16 *159*
3:19 *14*
3:22–4 *14*
3:24 *160*
4 *9*
6:5–6 *9*
6:11 *5, 145*
11:1–9 *9*
11:30 *9*
12:2–3 *9*
12:3 *38*
15:13 *15*
17:2 *10*
17:6–7 *10*
17:9–14 *124*
17:15–19 *8*
17:16 *51*
17:17 *9*
17:19 *10*
18:7 *10*
18:12 *10*
18:19 *127*
22:17 *51*
22:18 *38, 39*
26:4 *38*
30:13 *43*
31:1 *117*
32:1, 3 *85*
35:19 *78*
37:2 *14*
37:9 *157–8*
45:5 *14*
45:13 *117*
46:30 *125*
46:34 *112*
49:8 *51*
49:10 *28, 159*
49:10–11 *24*
49:26 *38*

Exodus
1:6–14 *15*
1:17–21 *16*
1:22 – 2:10 *13*
2:1–10 *15*
3 *17*
6:6 *67, 126*
6:20 *15*
13:2 *124*
15:10 *67*
15:19 *67*
15:20 *15*
16 *19*
16:12 *18, 22*
19:4 *158*
19:5–6 *38*
24 *17*
30:6 *100*

Index of Scripture references

Leviticus
12:8 *107*
15:31 *38*
18:12 *15*
22:2 *38*
25:5–11 *38*
25:49 *146*

Numbers
6 *37–8*
8:25 *116*
22 *26*
22:7 *27*
22:31 *27*
23:11 *27*
23:23 *27*
24:10 *27*
24:15–19 *23*
24:17 *28, 51, 159*
25:1–13 *66–7*
25:13 *86*
26:59 *15*

Deuteronomy
6 *17*
18:15–19 *30*
32:4 *127*
33:5 *32*
34:9 *31*
34:10–12 *31*

Joshua
6:17 *85*
6:25 *85*
13:22 *27*

Judges
4:5 *78*
11:30–5 *110*
13:2–3 *10*
13:3–5 *35*
13:5 *10, 36, 37*
13:5–7 *10*
13:6 *36*
13:7 *39, 40*
13:8 *36, 73*
13:18 *37*
13:22 *36*
13:23 *37*
21:25 *110*

1 Samuel
1:4 *11*
1:5 *10, 43*
1:11 *11*
1:17 *11*
1:19 *78*
2:1 *43–4*
2:1–10 *41–2*
2:2–5 *44*
2:5 *45*
2:6–7 *151*
2:6–8 *46*
2:8 *53*
2:8–10 *46*
2:9 *51*
2:10 *102*
2:11 *43, 78*
2:21 *45*
3 *11*
7:17 *78*
8:5 *47*
10:1 *47*
10:2 *78*
16:19 *85*
25:1 *78*
29:4 *26*

2 Samuel
5:11 *85*
5:12 *51*
6:2 *51*
7:1 *51*
7:2–3 *51*
7:5–7 *51–2*
7:6–12 *52*
7:11–16 *49, 53*
7:13 *53*
7:14 *53–4*
7:15 *53*

Index of Scripture references

7:16 *53*
7:18–19 *52*
8:1–12 *27*
19:22 *26*

2 Kings
2:11–12 *160*
4:9–10 *107–8*
6:17 *160*
15:29 *59*
17:24 *59*

1 Chronicles
1:1 *5*
6:32 *134*
18:1–13 *27*

2 Chronicles
20:22–3 *27*

Nehemiah
13:29 *86*

Esther
1:1 *157*
2:15 *157*
2:17 *157*
9 *157*

Job
1 – 2 *5*
14:1–2 *145*
25:4 *145*
38:17 *58*

Psalms
1:1–6 *74*
2 *159*
19:1 *117*
23:4 *58, 139*
72 *28*
72:17 *43*
78:56 *135*
78:60–2 *135*
93:1 *112*
107:2 *139*
107:10–16 *140*
111:9 *126*
130:3–4 *146*
130:7–8 *146*
139:6 *37*
143:11–12 *74*

Proverbs
6:34 *66*

Ecclesiastes
7:15 *116*

Song of Songs
2:3 *70*

Isaiah
6:3 *117*
7:13–17 *96*
7:14 *95*
7:14–17 *11, 59*
8:3–4 *59*
8:12–15 *60*
8:16 *61*
8:20–2 *61*
9:1 *61*
9:1–7 *56–7*
9:2 *50, 65, 164*
9:3 *139*
9:6 *37, 145*
9:7 *66*
26:17–19 *158*
28:16 *61*
42:7 *126*
42:16 *127*
44:22 *103*
49:6 *134*
49:9 *126*
52:3 *103*
52:10 *125*
53:5–6 *54*
57:1 *116*
58 *63, 64*
59:1–2 *64*

Index of Scripture references

59:2 *103*
59:4–8 *64*
59:8 *126*
59:9 *73*
59:9–15 *64–5*
59:11 *73*
59:15–20 *65–6*
59:19 *67, 73*
59:20 *63, 67, 103*
59:21 *68*
60:1–7 *62, 63*
60:6 *67*
60:12 *68*
60:16 *68*
60:18 *68*
60:20 *68*
62:1–2 *118*
62:11–12 *118*
63:1–2 *24*
63:3–4 *25*
63:5 *25*
66:10–16 *119–20*

Jeremiah
7:25–6 *81*
15:15 *73*
17:1–4 *71–2*
17:5–8 *69*
17:9 *73*
17:11 *71*
17:13 *72, 73*
17:17–18 *73*
23:4–6 *112*
29:18 *39*
30:4–24 *80*
30:7–9 *80*
31:7 *82*
31:9 *97*
31:10–14 *78–9*
31:15 *76*
31:16–17 *79, 97*
31:31–4 *81–2*
31:34 *97*
40:1 *78*
44:8 *39*

Lamentations
3:37–8 *46*

Ezekiel
10 *160*
14:7 *38*
23:42 *157*

Daniel
8:10 *159*
10:6 *160*
10:12–13 *160*

Hosea
9:7 *78*
9:10 *38*
9:13 *76, 78*
13:14 *146*

Joel
2:28 *97*

Amos
2:11–12 *38*
3:6 *46*

Micah
4:9–10 *159*
5:3–4 *96*
5:15 *96*

Haggai
2:6–9 *120*

Zechariah
8:13 *39*
9:9 *26*
9:11 *26*

Malachi
1:6 *86*
1:14 *90*
2:2–4 *86*
2:5–6 *90*
2:5–8 *86*

Index of Scripture references

2:13–17 *86*
2:17 – 3:2 *84*
3:1 *86, 100*
3:3–5 *87*
3:7 *87*
4:1 *87*
4:5–6 *87*
4:6 *90*

NEW TESTAMENT

Matthew
1:1 *93*
1:16 *93*
1:18–25 *92*
1:20–1 *36*
1:22–3 *11, 95*
2:1–12 *28*
2:6 *96*
2:9 *50*
2:11 *67*
2:12 *77, 96*
2:13 *16*
2:13–14 *50*
2:13–15 *77, 94*
2:15 *16*
2:16 *16, 94*
2:16–18 *77*
2:17–18 *40*
2:18 *97*
2:19–23 *95*
2:20 *16*
2:21–3 *39*
2:23 *40*
3:2 *89*
3:13–14 *124*
3:15 *124*
4:12 *89*
4:12–14 *59*
5:3–11 *101*
5:17 *125*
7:24–7 *32*
9:6 *90*
11:9 *88*
11:10 *88*
11:14 *88*
15:10 *32*
15:38 – 16:1 *20*
16:5–12 *20*
16:14 *90*
16:25 *152*
17:2 *88*
17:11–13 *88*
19:26 *145*
19:28 *120*
21:1–7 *26*
26:71 *40*

Mark
1:1 *99*
1:1–4 *88–9*
1:4 *90*
1:14–15 *89*
3:33–4 *16–17*
6:3 *45*
6:7 *90*
6:12 *90*
8:38 *90*
14:36 *19*
14:67 *40*

Luke
1:1 *99*
1:3 *94*
1:5 *89, 99*
1:5–56 *127*
1:5 – 2:52 *116*
1:6 *100*
1:7 *116*
1:8–9 *100*
1:11 *100*
1:15 *100*
1:16–17 *89*
1:20 *100*
1:25 *101*
1:26 *94*
1:26–38 *36*
1:32 *37*
1:32–3 *111*
1:34 *111, 116*

173

Index of Scripture references

1:36 *100*
1:39 *94, 107*
1:41–5 *101*
1:46–8 *43*
1:46–55 *43, 102*
1:48–9 *43–4*
1:49–53 *44*
1:51–2 *102*
1:54–5 *45*
1:56 *94*
1:62 *100*
1:64 *101*
1:67 *101, 115*
1:68 *126*
1:68–79 *47, 98*
1:69 *126*
1:74–5 *127*
1:76 *117*
1:79 *126*
1:80 *117*
2:3 *108*
2:4 *94, 107*
2:6 *94, 107*
2:7 *107, 108*
2:8 *50, 116*
2:8–20 *105*
2:8–14 *114*
2:9 *120*
2:13 *112, 116*
2:14 *113, 117, 120, 134*
2:17–18 *4*
2:20 *111*
2:21–3 *124*
2:22 *94*
2:22–4 *107*
2:25 *125*
2:26 *116*
2:27–35 *123*
2:31 *125*
2:34–5 *128*
2:37–8 *126*
2:38 *4, 126*
2:39 *94*
2:41 *95*
2:44 *107*

2:46 *128*
2:47 *117*
3:6 *125*
4:18 *90*
4:36 *90*
4:43 *90*
6:20–2 *101*
7:28 *90*
8:8 *128*
8:18 *32*
9:16 *101*
9:31 *26*
10:34 *107*
12:27 *118*
13:15 *108*
14:35 *128*
16:16 *4*
16:24–5 *128*
19:38 *117*
20:17 *47, 61*
22:11–12 *107*
22:43 *160*
23:54–6 *141*
24:21 *102, 128*
24:26 *119*
24:30 *101*
24:44 *4*
24:47–8 *103*

John
1 *133, 156*
1:1–3 *33, 133*
1:1–14 *129*
1:4–5 *139*
1:5 *50*
1:7 *133, 136*
1:9 *133*
1:10–11 *135*
1:12 *134*
1:14 *17, 33, 53, 133, 134, 138, 139*
1:15 *133*
1:18 *133*
1:45 *4, 16*
2:4 *16*
2:18 *138*

Index of Scripture references

2:23 *138*
3:2 *140*
3:2–15 *138*
3:16 *138*
3:16–21 *137*
3:17 *7, 34, 138*
3:19 *139*
3:19–20 *139*
3:31–6 *33*
4:5–10 *164–5*
5:22–7 *33*
5:24 *90*
6 *21*
6:26–7 *21–2*
6:28 *19*
6:30–1 *19*
6:32–5 *19*
6:33 *21*
6:35 *18, 21*
6:38–40 *19, 138*
6:40 *21*
6:41–2 *19*
6:49–51 *19*
6:52–8 *20*
6:54 *21*
6:55–8 *20*
6:63 *21*
7:26–51 *140*
8:12 *139*
8:26 *32*
8:28 *32*
8:34–6 *147*
8:50 *120*
10:10 *14, 90*
11:25 *152*
12:14–16 *26*
14:3 *90*
18:37 *136*
19:26–7 *17*
19:31 *141*
19:38–42 *141*

Acts
2:24 *144*
2:38 *90*
2:38–9 *103–4*
3:15 *144*
3:20–2 *32*
3:24–6 *147*
5:29 *131*
10:42–3 *104*
13:38–9 *104*
16:35–9 *153*
17:6 *48*
19:4 *90*
21:20 *127*
22:11 *118*
24:5 *39*
26:2 *101*
28:28 *125*

Romans
2:9–10 *119*
2:15 *6*
3:12 *6*
3:21 *145*
4:11 *124*
5:12 *3, 5, 54*
5:17 *54–5*
5:19 *5*
6:17–18 *153*
7:19 *7*
7:24–5 *7*
8:3 *157*
8:9–11 *135*
8:15 *19*
8:17 *136, 153*
8:18 *119*
13:5 *131*

1 Corinthians
3:16 *135*
15:22 *5*
15:42–4 *153*
15:43 *119*
15:45 *5*
16:22 *74*

2 Corinthians
2:15–16 *136*

Index of Scripture references

4:6 *61*
4:17 *119*
5:21 *54, 145, 151*
6:2 *125*
8:9 *151*

Galatians
3:13 *90*
3:13–14 *157*
4:4–7 *143*
4:5 *150*
4:6 *19*
4:7 *147*

Ephesians
2:22 *55*
3:13 *119*
5:23 *136*
5:29–30 *136*
6:12 *160–1*

Philippians
1:29 *154*
2:3–4 *153*
2:5–8 *149, 150*
2:8 *161, 162*
2:20 *153*
3:10–11 *153*
3:17 *153*

Colossians
1:15 *136, 163*
1:18 *136, 163*
1:21–2 *151*
1:24 *154*
1:24–7 *136*
2:9 *154*
2:9–10 *134*
3:12 *112*

1 Timothy
1:15–17 *166*
3:6–7 *5*
3:11 *5*
3:16 *151*

2 Timothy
1:9–10 *152*
2:26 *5*
3:3 *5*

Titus
2:11 *125*
3:7 *147*

Hebrews
1:1–2 *97*
2:10 *119*
2:14–17 *150*
2:15 *153*
2:17 *154*
9:12 *126*
10:25 *131*
11:7 *147*
11:24 *16*

1 Peter
1:2 *153–4*
1:11 *119*
2:22 *145*
3:7 *147*
4:13 *119, 153*

2 Peter
2:15 *27*
2:16 *26*

1 John
3:8 *163*
4:9 *9, 11*

Jude
11 *27*
14 *5*

Revelation
1:5 *161*
2:14 *27*
5:9 *127, 161*
12:1–6 *155*
12:7–8 *161*

Index of Scripture references

12:9 *159*
12:10–12 *162*
12:11 *161*
12:12 *134*
12:14 *158, 161*
12:17 *158, 161, 163*
13:6 *134*
14:6–7 *121*
14:19–20 *25*

19:11–15 *25*
19:13 *33*
19:13–16 *37*
21:3 *53*
22:2 *74*
22:16 *28*
22:16–17 *164*
22:20 *73*

Index of non-biblical names

Alexander, Cecil Frances 110
Anderson, Neil 167
Athanasius 134

Bailey, Ken 167
Barr, James 16
Bejon, James 167
Blaylock, Richard 167
Blowers, Paul 132
Blumenfeld, Bruno 135

Cappeau, Placide 165
Capra, Frank 1
Chapian, Marie 109
Como, David 132
Cox, Rory 131, 132
Croteau, David 112

Dalman, Gustaf Hermann 109
Deir 'Alla 27
Dickens, Charles 71
Dix, William Chatterton 55
Drummond, Henry 2

Eames, Christopher 9

Feliciano, José 70, 74

Gandhi, Mahatma 6
Girolami, Remigio de' 131
Grosseteste, Robert 132

Hooker, Morna 132, 152, 167
Humphreys, C. J. 50

Irenaeus 152

Johnston, George 144

Kent, John 162
King Jr, Martin Luther 147
Kolbe, Fr Maximilian 146
Kronstadt, St John of 151–2
Kubrick, Stanley 156

Lahey, Stephen 132
Luther, Martin 71

MacArthur, John 131
Maximus Confessor 132
May, Mike 152
McCracken, Brett 130, 132

Need, Stephen 132
Northrup, Bernard 52

O'Donovan, Oliver 134

Pannenberg, Wolfhart 133
Paul, Ian 108
Petterson, Anthony 167
Pickering, Jeff 131

Salleron, Louis 132
Sears, Edmund 121
Smith, George Adam 2

Teresa, Mother 6
Thomson, William McClure 109
Tikkanen, Amy 71
Tolkien, J. R. R. 156
Troeltsch, Ernst 5

Wachowskis 156
Wadding, Luke 142
Ward, Graham 135
Watts, Isaac 91
Workman, Herbert 132